HELPING ABUSED CHILDREN AND THEIR FAMILIES

Towards an evidence-based practice model

Chris Trotter

Dr Chris Trotter is Associate Professor in Social Work at Monash University and is also author of *Working With Involuntary Clients: A Guide to Practice*, published by Sage Publications. He can be contacted for videos and seminars on **chris.trotter@med.monash.edu.au**

⑤SAGE Publications
London • Thousand Oaks • New Delhi

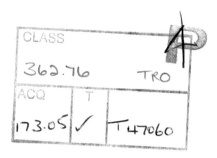
© Chris Trotter 2004

First published in 2004 by
Allen & Unwin
83 Alexander St
Crows Nest NSW 2065
Australia

SAGE Publications Ltd
1 Oliver's Yard
55 City Road
London EC1Y 1SP

SAGE Publications Inc.
2455 Teller Road
Thousand Oaks, California 91320

SAGE Publications India Pvt Ltd
B-42, Panchsheel Enclave
Post Box 4109
New Delhi 100 017

British Library Cataloguing in Publication data

A catalogue record for this book is available from the British Library

ISBN 1 4129 0354 8
ISBN 1 4129 0355 6 (pbk)

Library of Congress Control Number: 2004102656

Typeset by Bookhouse, Sydney
Printed in Singapore by South Wind Production

ACKNOWLEDGMENTS

I wish to acknowledge the assistance of numerous people who have contributed to this book. The research project on which the book is based was initiated by the late Robin Clark, the Director of Child Protection in Victoria. Lynn McPherson, Manager of Child Protection Training, Pat Semmens, the regional Child Protection Manager, and Peter Green, the current director, supported the project from the outset and were a key part of its success. Jan Mumford worked tirelessly for two years interviewing more than 300 workers and clients. Particular thanks must go to the staff and clients in child protection in the Eastern Region of the Department of Human Services for their participation in the study. Louise Oliaro and Peter Hiller spent many hours classifying the data and entering it into the computer. Elizabeth Weiss from Allen & Unwin has been exceptionally patient and helped a lot with the way the book developed. Thanks also to Alex Nahlous for editorial assistance. Thanks go also to my colleagues in the Social Work Department at Monash University, particularly Rosemary Sheehan, Delia O'Donohue and Lesley Hewitt, who gave me feedback on early drafts. Particular thanks must go to Michael Clanchy, Judith Gibbs, Robbie Gilligan, Judith Burton and Agi O'Hara who provided valuable comments on the final draft. Thanks also to the Australian Research Council which, with Monash University and the Department of Human Services Victoria, funded the study. And finally thanks to my family, Joan, David, Rebecca and Moo for their support.

v

CONTENTS

CHILD PROTECTION IN CRISIS?

I had visited Mr Pope for some months and I knew I should focus on my relationship skills. We should be working together—in partnership. I had read enough to know that the big stick approach did not work.

But I also knew he had hit his two-year-old child on two occasions, once so severely that she had to be admitted to hospital. And he seemed to show little, if any, remorse for what he had done. I was also being told by my supervisor that protection of the child from further abuse was my primary responsibility. How was I supposed to work in partnership and protect the child? How could I get him to understand that hitting his child not only damaged her physically but would also cause irreparable long-term damage to her.

I was never quite sure what I was supposed to say to him. Should I be reminding him of the damage he could do, telling him about other children who had been killed by their parents, confronting him about his lack of understanding and remorse? Or should I be working in partnership? Did this mean accepting his twisted perspective? What was it exactly that I could say and do to make little Sophie safer?

I was also expected to conduct an ongoing risk assessment. If the risk continued to be high we would have to go back to court to have an order made so I could keep seeing the family. Somehow I was supposed to work in partnership with Mr Pope, be open about my role and purpose, but also find out whether he was lying to me about how he was treating Sophie. In order to get the information to protect Sophie I could not be completely open about what I was doing. I had to visit without warning, catch him off guard, or encourage him to give himself away. Anyway it never seemed like partnership.

I was also never quite sure how I was supposed to be helping this family with their problems. I had persuaded Mr Pope to start seeing a social worker at United Family Services. The social worker was trying to get him into a parenting skills group. A nurse from the Deparment of Health was also visiting several times a week again in an attempt to help Mr Pope with caring for Sophie. The other workers seemed to be in the partnership but I didn't.

These words, uttered by Margaret, who has worked in child protection for some years, reflect the dilemma which so many professionals face in child protection and child welfare work. How do you work in partnership and simultaneously assess risk and exercise authority?

This book is about how Margaret and other child protection workers can help people like Mr Pope to provide better care for their children. It is about how you can help children and their parents in what have often become proceduralised and forensic child protection systems. It is about what works and what doesn't.

There are of course many instances when the best interests of children are served by removing them from their families. The focus of this book is not, however, about making decisions regarding whether or not children should be removed. It is more about how to work with families and children, where the families are together but there continues to be ongoing child protection concerns.

The book is about work in government child protection services. It is, however, also relevant to those who work with abused children in voluntary agencies or family support programs.

I have used the term 'client' to refer to parents, children or carers who are involved in the child protection system. It is acknowledged, however, that the interests of an abused child are often very different to those of a parent. In fact it is often argued that the child or young person who has been abused or neglected should be viewed as the client. So while I have used 'client' to describe all service recipients I have tried throughout the book to distinguish between two types of clients—clients who are parents or carers (and in many cases perpetrators) and clients who are children or young people who have been the victims of child abuse and neglect.

The media gaze

For the past two decades the field of child protection has been full of controversy. In the words of one American commentator,

> Fifty years ago the nation's press would not cover the story of mistreated children at all, because it was 'indecent'. Twenty-five years ago, investigative reporters began climbing all over the story, but mostly for its shock and scandal value. Today . . . they are still limited by space and vision. (Levey 1999: 997)

There have been a number of high-profile cases in which children have died despite the involvement of social workers and other helping professionals. One of the most well-known examples is the case of Maria Colwell in the United Kingdom. Maria, at the age of six months, was placed in foster care because of neglect by her mother. At the age of six years she was returned to her mother and stepfather under court supervision. About nine months later she was beaten to death by her stepfather. Between the time she was placed with her mother and stepfather and her death she was visited on 56 occasions by child protection workers and other professionals, and 30 complaints were made about her care. Each of the professionals involved assumed that someone else was providing the primary service to the family (Howells 1974).

The Daniel Valerio case in Australia was similar. Daniel was murdered by his de facto father in 1990. At the time of his death he had 104 bruises on his body and two fractured collarbones which had started to heal despite the fact that he had received no treatment for them. In the three months before his death, Daniel had been seen by more than 20 professionals, including doctors, social workers, medical specialists, police and community workers. Each of those who visited was suspicious that he was a victim of child abuse. None of them, however, took action to remove Daniel from the family or to protect him from his father.

In these and in other high-profile cases individual social workers have often been severely criticised by the courts and the press. When Kim Anne Poden, a nineteen-month-old child under the supervision of the Children's Aid Society in Canada, died of head injuries in 1976, the judge was highly critical of the way the case was handled by the Children's Aid Society. A subsequent judicial inquiry placed much of the blame at the feet of individual social workers.

These cases led the courts, the press, children's welfare organisations, government departments and politicians to question the systems that allowed these deaths to happen. They also led to an increasing interest in and awareness of the dangers of child abuse.

The ethical and value-based nature of child protection work has also come under scrutiny. One very good example of this is the high-profile debate which has raged in Australian newspapers in recent years about whether or not the Australian nation should apologise to the stolen generation—those children who, a generation ago, were forcibly removed from their families simply because they were Aboriginal. Similar debates have been seen in relation to North America's indigenous populations.

Anthony McMahon (1998) in his book, *Damned if you do, Damned if you don't*, suggests that public interest in child abuse has been further fuelled in the United States by the involvement of high-profile media identities. Oprah Winfrey, for example, publicly acknowledged that she had been raped as a child.

No doubt, as a result of this growing interest in child protection there has been an expansion in many western countries of government child protection and child welfare services. Alongside this expansion there has been a dramatic increase in the numbers of child protection reports, in many cases as a direct result of the introduction of mandatory reporting systems which require professionals who work with children to report instances of abuse to child protection authorities. In the decade between the mid-1980s and the mid-1990s most English-speaking countries saw increases in reports of child abuse of more than 200 per cent. The United States today sees something like three million reports a year. So despite the increase in services the ability of the system to investigate and deal with these reports is often compromised (Department of Health and Human Services [US] 2001). And the high-profile child protection 'failures' have continued to occur.

The Climbie case in the United Kingdom is an example. In 2001, Victoria Climbie, in the words of Lord Laming who conducted an inquiry into her murder, spent the cold winter months prior to her death

> bound hand and foot, in an unheated bathroom, lying in the cold bath in a plastic bag in her own urine and faeces and having to eat what food she could get by pressing her face onto the plate of whatever was put in the bath beside her. (Laming 2003: 2)

Yet Victoria had been known in the ten months before her death to 'no fewer than 4 social service departments, 3 housing departments, two specialist child protection teams in the metropolitan police, she had been admitted to 2 different hospitals and referred to the National Society for Protection of Children'. The most striking feature of the case was the 'sheer number of occasions when the most minor and basic intervention on the part of the staff concerned could have made a material difference to the eventual outcome'.

Child protection—helping or social control?

The development of child protection systems in English-speaking countries over the past two decades has been paralleled by an increasing focus on what might be termed forensic or investigatory approaches to child protection work. Services are more and more characterised by a focus on whether abuse has occurred and, if so, the likelihood that it will be repeated. If it is found that abuse has occurred then this might lead to a notification becoming substantiated or the family concerned being placed on a child protection register. Most services now routinely use risk assessment processes that aim to determine which cases are high risk and therefore need immediate attention.

The risk assessment process provides a method of dealing with the increases in referrals. Scarce resources can be devoted to high-risk and substantiated referrals. Low-risk and unsubstantiated cases can be left alone. There are, however, many critics of the current systems. It is argued that they are legalistic, they focus on surveillance rather than welfare and they do not achieve the very purpose for which they have been set up—to protect children from harm. It is argued that most of the energy of child protection services is directed towards risk assessment rather than treatment, and it is hardly surprising that families and children are not being helped (Jack 1997; Gough 1993; Krane and Davies 2000; Parton, Thorpe and Wattam 1997). In the words of Anne Cohn Donelly (1999: 990) in relation to the American system, 'Victims rarely get what is needed to repair the hurt and break the cycle.'

There is certainly some evidence for this view. A study by Elaine Farmer (1999) examined case planning meetings in the United Kingdom in the early 1990s. She found that the meetings focused primarily on risk issues and whether children should be placed on the child protection register. Only about fifteen per cent of the time was spent discussing treatment plans for the children and their families. A study by Gray and colleagues (1997) also in the United Kingdom suggested that clients feel they get little in the way of treatment from statutory child protection services. They suggest that clients feel there are gaps in services and workers are often out of touch.

David Gough (1993: 21) in an extensive review of research on the effectiveness of child protection suggests that child protection services have contributed little in terms of improved outcomes for children: 'There is little evidence that child protection services improve outcomes for children or reduce re-referral rates (except where children are permanently removed).'

It seems that the pressure felt by Margaret in the case example referred to earlier—the pressure to establish the extent and nature of the abuse and to assess risk—is reflected in the practice and the organisation of many child protection services around the world.

The critics of child protection services in the United Kingdom have pointed to the different nature of services in Western Europe. British, North American and Australian child protection services are characterised by many layers of command. A senior child protection worker reports to a team leader, who reports to a child protection manager, who reports to a regional manager and so on. Most important decisions, even decisions to continue working with a family, are taken by someone up the hierarchy, whereas child protection services in Europe tend to have flatter management structures and give more responsibility to the frontline workers. Decisions, even decisions to remove children from the home, may be the ultimate responsibility of the child protection workers themselves. The focus of this type of child protection intervention is on helping the family with their problems, rather than determining whether abuse has occurred or the risk of future abuse. In only rare instances are children taken to court (Heatherington et al. 1997; Littlechild 1998).

This approach is well illustrated in a child protection service I visited in Austria. The child protection workers, rather than refer to other agencies or other expert workers, would seek advice from expert panels. Those panels might include medical staff, drug and alcohol experts and other advisers and they would help the worker to work with the family. They would also help the worker to make decisions such as whether or not a family should be taken to court. The system provides for maximum continuity of contact between one worker and one client, something which does not occur in the more specialised case management or contracting models which operate in most English-speaking countries.

The difference between the European and British systems is characterised by comments reputed to have been made by two child protection workers on initial visits to a mother and father suspected of child abuse. The British child protection worker commented: 'We have had a report that you have been harming your children and I am here to investigate this.' The European child protection worker on the other hand commented: 'I have heard that you might be having some trouble with your children and I am here to see if I can help you with them or with any other problems you might have.'

Critics of the British system in particular have argued that their child protection services should be more like the European services. They should focus more on welfare and less on risk assessment (e.g. Littlechild 1998; Heatherington et al. 1997). They argue that it is not possible to distinguish between high-risk and low-risk cases in the early stages and that the divisions are artificial. It is pointed out that in the vast majority of cases children remain with their families and the focus on risk assessment diverts child protection workers from helping those children and their families.

Others have argued that cases should be moved away from the child protection services into voluntary services where families receive welfare rather than investigatory services. According to David Thorpe,

> There are children who are the victims of serious neglect, physical or sexual assaults. They require protection and approximately ten per cent of children drawn into the mouth of the child protection net will filter down into this category. The use of emotive

words such as abuse, maltreatment and perpetrator should be confined to those cases. (1994: 202)

It seems, however, that despite the increased focus on the investigatory function and despite the arguments that child protection services are now too investigatory, some commentators in the popular press are still not satisfied. As I mentioned earlier new child protection 'failures' continue to be publicised usually with the suggestion that child protection workers failed to assess the situation adequately.

There is also some recent criticism by academics of child protection assessment processes. Janet Stanley and Chris Goddard (2002), for example, argue that sometimes child protection workers underestimate the levels of abuse in families because they feel intimidated and threatened by parents. In other words children are not protected because the child protection workers do not focus sufficiently on their protective function. They point to initiatives by the New Zealand government as potential solutions to the problem. These initiatives include dangerous situations teams, independent reviews and fast tracking of access to specialist services.

The controversy about the role of child protection is ongoing. High-profile criticism of child protection failures has led to an increase in investigatory approaches. This has in turn led to criticism of the new focus on investigatory approaches. Despite this, however, the adequacy of the investigatory approaches continues to be questioned.

Case management

Child protection services in English-speaking countries for the most part work on a case management system. In other words, welfare services are managed and co-ordinated by case managers— usually child protection workers employed by government departments. Most of the helping or treatment services are then provided by voluntary agencies. This system is sometimes referred to in terms of a purchaser/provider separation—case managers purchase, or enlist the assistance of service providers, on behalf of their clients (Hood 1997).

So the child protection workers are responsible for co-ordinating welfare or helping services rather than providing these services themselves. Individual clients within the child protection system, whether parents or children, could be seeing a family support worker, a school welfare worker, a psychologist, a drug counsellor, a domestic violence counsellor, or a court advice worker. A parent could also be involved with a financial counsellor, a parent support group, or a domestic violence counselling group.

The extent to which this occurs varies within and between different countries. Christine Hallett (1995), for example, found in a British study that child protection workers did much of the direct work with children and families themselves. Hood (1997), on the other hand, found in a study of United Kingdom local authorities that while there was a lot of good work done in the view of the staff concerned, the practice of referring and contracting out led to concerns about the mis-communication of information, duplication of roles, role confusion and de-skilling and disempowering of workers. The statutory workers often felt de-skilled as helpers. They often felt they did not know families well enough to make decisions about them. Workers in the voluntary agencies, on the other hand, often felt disempowered in terms of decision making.

A study undertaken in Illinois in the United States confirms the sense of disempowerment experienced by workers. One of the workers quoted said, 'When I first came here it was more a personal kind of counselling. Now . . . you just meet them and say that you need to go to a counsellor.' (McMahon 1998: 38) This theme is also supported by Skehill and colleagues (1999) in an Irish study. They found that while there was generally good communication between workers and agencies, there was some role confusion and statutory workers were uncomfortable with their central role, particularly when they had minimal involvement with the family.

There does, therefore, appear to be a view held by at least some of those involved in the child protection system that the practice of referral and contracting can be problematic. I argued in my earlier book (Trotter 1999) that effective work with involuntary clients involves ongoing contact between worker and client, and that early interviews, when risk assessment takes place, provide the perfect opportunity to begin a helping or therapeutic process.

I have also argued, along with others (e.g. Jones and Alcabes 1993), that the skills of work with involuntary clients are largely generic ones and that holistic approaches are most effective. In other words, there are advantages in having one worker who understands her or his clients in a broad context and who helps those clients work through a range of issues which are of concern to them. When a client sees several professionals in relation to multiple problems the client may be required to repeat her or his story over and over. Not only would this be tiresome but it might also lead to poorer outcomes given the time it takes to develop an effective client/worker relationship.

Direct practice skills vary little whether the client is a drug user, has mental illness or is a criminal offender. Jones and Alcabes (1993) argue on the basis of the available research that in work with clients in any of these fields the key to effective practice relates to socialisation processes, including role clarification and reaching agreement on problem definition and goals. This process takes time and may never occur if clients are exposed to repeated short-term contacts with different specialist workers. In other words, there is an inevitable overlap of services if each of the workers makes use of effective practices.

The intervention by the drug counsellor, the child protection worker, the mental health social worker or the family support worker will all involve a holistic assessment of the clients' situation, the development of goals and the strategies to achieve them. The more successful interventions treat the person in their context, not the symptom or the problem. The concept of specialised services may be an extremely valuable one in health where there are more specific specialisations and roles are clearer, however, in child protection it may lead to fragmentation and discontinuity of service with poorer outcomes for clients.

Evidence-based practice

It is apparent that child protection work in English-speaking countries has, in recent times, become increasingly complex. It is increasingly politicised and subject to media interest. The numbers of child protection workers have increased but the volume of notifications and workloads have increased even more. Child protection services are increasingly concerned about whether abuse has occurred and with risk assessment processes. And there is an increasing tendency for welfare services to be provided by voluntary agencies as more and more of the direct service work is contracted out—often leading to an increasing fragmentation of services.

Is it possible in this environment to do effective work? Can child protection workers help parents to be less abusive or young people to be less self-destructive? Can they help to keep families and children together? Can they provide services which clients are happy with and which they feel are helpful?

Before answering these questions another question immediately arises: Can we tell if services are effective or not?

There is a divergence of views among both academics and practitioners on this issue. Some support the notion of evidence-based or empirical practice. They argue that it is possible and desirable to measure the effectiveness of different programs and direct-practice approaches and they argue that interventions should be based on the findings of effectiveness research. Others argue that the concept of evidence-based practice is flawed.

What is evidence-based practice?

Let's look at the case example discussed earlier in this chapter. Should Margaret confront Mr Pope? Should she simply focus on his abusive behaviour or try to help him with issues which might not be directly related to his abusive behaviour? Should she try to help Mr Pope with deep-seated issues he has with his own family of origin and the abusive environment in which he was raised? Is there any point trying to engage him in a helping relationship at all? In making this decision Margaret can simply rely on her professional judgment. Alternatively, if she were to adopt an evidence-based practice approach she would look to the research about what has worked best in these situations in the past.

A number of studies have been undertaken which have examined the use of particlar types of interventions and how these relate to client outcomes. For example a study by Laurence Shulman (1991) undertaken in Canada asked clients a range of questions about their workers; for example, did the worker help them to clarify the purpose of the intervention, did the worker help to put their feelings into words, did the worker break down their concerns into manageable parts. Shulman found that when the workers did these things their clients felt that their workers were helpful, they were less likely to go to court and they had fewer days in care, compared to when workers did not do these things. Other studies have also found that when child protection workers have particular skills their clients do better (see Trotter 1999 for a review of these studies).

What does this mean for a worker like Margaret? It means, if she adopts an evidence-based practice approach she will firstly engage Mr Pope in a helping intervention because she has some confidence that she may be able to help Mr Pope and Sophie in some tangible way. She will then spend time exploring with Mr Pope the purpose of the intervention, what he hopes to gain from it and what she hopes to gain from it. She will also try to understand and put into words how he feels about his situation and she will try to identify and define the things he is concerned or worried about.

She will be very clear about her expectations of Mr Pope and she will carefully monitor Sophie's situation and progress. She will do these things because the research evidence suggests they are

likely to be effective. She may, however, be cautious about using confrontation, particularly early in her work with Mr Pope, on the basis of the small number of studies which have suggested that confrontation is not likely to be succesful in changing a client's behaviour unless there is a strong client/worker relationship (e.g. Lieberman, Yalom and Miles 1973; Shulman 1991). She may also be cautious about undertaking an in-depth exploration of Mr Pope's family of origin on the basis that some research has pointed to the value of working on the current situation with realistic and achievable goals (e.g. Shulman 1991; Smokowski and Wodarski 1996).

Criticisms and counter-criticisms of evidence-based practice

There has been much criticism of evidence-based practice (e.g. Ife 1997; Pease and Fook 1999; Webb 2001). This book is based, however, on the assumption that evidence-based practice is a legitimate approach to child protection work and for this reason I will attempt to counter some of the criticisms.

It is argued that outcome measures mean little and are often contradictory. The following case study illustrates the complexity of assessing effectiveness in child protection.

Brent lived with Bridgit and their three children for several years until the relationship broke down. Shortly after that time Bridgit began using drugs heavily and child protection removed the children and placed them in temporary foster care. The child protection worker took the case to court and a court order was made giving custody of the children to the Child Protection Service. The children were then placed with Brent.

The child protection worker was interviewed some months later and was very happy with the progress of the children. When asked to rate the overall progress of the children and their progress in relation to the presenting problem she was very positive. Brent was also interviewed. He also believed the children were progressing well. Brent had a high opinion of the child protection worker. He described her as friendly, open, fair and a good supervisor. However, when asked to comment on how satisfied he was about the outcome of the child protection intervention he gave it a rating of 1 on a 7-point scale. In other words he was quite dissatisfied with the outcome. He believed child protection did little to keep the mother and the children together and if things had been handled differently—'more support and less attack'—the children might still be with their mother. In his words, 'there are now three kids without a mum'. The children themselves also had mixed feelings. They loved their father but missed their mother.

Has this family progressed well? Are the outcomes good? In this instance, as in many others, it is simply not possible to give a 'yes' or 'no' answer. Some outcomes are positive and some are not. It can be argued however, that this is not a reason not to measure outcomes, rather it points to the need to be cautious about interpreting outcome measures when they conflict with each other, and for research studies to use multiple outcome measures. This example illustrates that interventions may be partly effective and partly ineffective, not that evidence-based practice is flawed.

The opponents of evidence-based practice argue further that it is not possible to quantify the subjective realities of client's lives. That the attempt to develop measurable outcomes inevitably ignores hard to define concepts such as self-esteem or empowerment. It also ignores more macro objectives relating to social change and community development. In response to this argument it cannot be suggested that evidence-based practice provides all the answers. Nevertheless, some things can be measured and it is valuable to measure them. Perhaps the challenge for evidence-based practice is to try to capture some of the more elusive concepts, such as empowerment.

Opponents of evidence-based practice often argue that each client situation is uniquely individual; it is not possible to generalise

from one situation to another. However, much of the research in child protection and in other welfare settings suggests there is often consistency across populations and individual situations. For example, the defining of client goals seems to be related to positive outcomes in many studies in many different settings (Andrews et al. 1979; Jones and Alcabes 1993; O'Hare 1991; Reid 1997; Reid and Hanrahan 1981; Rubin 1985; Sheldon 1987; Trotter 1993, 1996; Videka Sherman 1988). There appear to be few, if any, studies that have examined this concept and have not found it to be related to positive outcomes. Perhaps the argument about the unique individuality of the client group simply points to the need for more and more research in different settings so knowledge can be further developed about what works best in what situations.

Another argument which is presented by critics of evidence-based practice is that even if the outcomes are clearly and consistently positive, it may not be possible to determine what has led to the positive outcomes. How can you know whether it is the worker's intervention that has made the difference, rather than the myriad of other factors which may influence the lives of client families? Positive changes might have occurred as a result of the interest from a neighbour or a school teacher or simply by the resolve of family members.

On the other hand, research methodology is sufficiently sophisticated to give us a fair indication of the extent to which an intervention might have been responsible for the outcomes rather than other factors, such as the maturation of family members or a helpful neighbour.

When repeated studies with large samples continue to find particular approaches related to positive outcomes, it is likely there is a cause-and-effect relationship. This is even more likely if there is a theory which can explain the relationship. For example, the setting of client-defined goals is not only related to positive outcomes, its value is supported by motivational theories that suggest people are more likely to change if they work towards their own goals.

Finally, evidence-based practice may be criticised as being

based in the workers' or the researchers' value system. The questions which researchers ask and the outcome measures they use are not the clients' questions and outcome measures, and again they may not take account of the subjective realities of those clients' lives. On the other hand much of the more recent research is qualitative in nature and focuses on clients' subjective perceptions.

Why evidence-based practice?

Evidence-based practice clearly has its limitations. I am certainly not suggesting that research evidence is the only thing which should guide practice. The worker must, for example, take into account the expectations of her or his employing organisation. Workers also learn and change their behaviour as a result of their experiences with clients. They also should take into account various theories of human behaviour and different intervention models.

Research evidence cannot provide all the answers. I am arguing, however, that if workers adopt an evidence-based approach as their underlying practice paradigm they are likely to be more effective than if they rely only on other sources of knowledge, for example, practice wisdom or theories of behaviour.

Jill Gibbons in an argument in favour of evidence-based practice points to the fact that researchers have been doing outcome-based studies in child welfare dating back to 1922 (Gibbons 2001). More recently we continue to see pleas for more evidence-based work. Chadwick and colleagues (1999: 1015), for example, in a recent edition of *Child Abuse and Neglect* comment: 'Outcome studies are required to test the efficacy of remedies and practices—we need more data to know if what we have done for the past 25 years actually makes a difference.'

Perhaps the most persuasive argument in favour of evidence-based practice is that other methods of developing knowledge are likely to be more flawed than an evidence-based approach. If a worker relies solely on theories of behaviour or practice wisdom or professional judgment, then how can that worker know if she

or he is doing well or not. There are many examples of intervention programs in the human services with poor outcomes (e.g. Gough 1993). If they are not measured how can an individual worker know whether his or her work is resulting in good or poor outcomes?

In this book I have therefore accepted that evidence-based practice is a legitimate approach to work in child protection. The book rests on the assumption that an intervention is likely to be a better one if the worker believes the family has made good progress, if the client is happy with the worker and the outcome and feels that his or her problems have been reduced, if children have remained with their families, and if cases have been closed. While recognising the complexity of attempting to measure outcomes in child protection, it is assumed that an intervention is less likely to be effective if the worker feels the client has deteriorated, if the client is dissatisfied with the worker and the outcome, if the children have been removed from their family and if the case has remained open.

In other words, child protection interventions are better ones if workers and clients say they are good and if apparently concrete indications of progress, such as case closure, confirm the workers' and clients' views. The interventions are not so good if these different measures are equivocal or contradictory. They are worse if they are negative.

These outcome measures may not be a sign of effectiveness in every case, in fact, as discussed later in this chapter, cases being closed and children remaining at home may represent poor outcomes. Generally speaking, however, interventions which have apparently positive outcomes are likely to be better ones than those which have apparently negative outcomes.

(For a more detailed discussion about the criticisms and advantages of evidence-based practice the reader is refered to two articles published in the *British Journal of Social Work*—a critique by Stephen Webb [2001] and a defence by Brian Sheldon [2001].)

What works?

What does the research tell us about what works and what doesn't? One problem facing the evidence-based practitioner in child protection is the limited evidence about what works in routine child protection work. Many articles and a number of books examine the effectiveness of child welfare and child protection programs. Books such as those by David Gough (1993) and Anthony Maluccio and his colleagues (2000) provide very good reviews of the outcome research. The focus of most of the research is, however, specialist programs and services such as foster care or family preservation. Little has been done on the effectiveness of routine child protection services.

Geraldine Macdonald (2001) in her book, *Effective Interventions in Child Abuse and Neglect*, examines reviews of effectiveness studies in child protection. She identifies some research evidence in support of behavioural and cognitive behavioural programs, skills training, behavioural family work, modelling, problem solving and holistic care management. She could not, however, locate any studies that focused on routine child protection services (as opposed to specialist programs). She comments: ' . . . it is difficult to conclude anything other than that the available evidence base underpinning what I shall call therapeutic (as opposed to administrative or legal) interventions in child protection is wafer thin' (Macdonald 2001: 167).

There is some truth in this comment and the lack of evidence certainly presents a problem for the evidence-based practitioner. This book aims to go some way towards addressing the problem. There is, however, some research on routine child protection practices, such as Lawrence Shulman's (1991) book, *Interactional Social Work Practice*, which provides an excellent example even though it was written some time ago. There is also a substantial body of research which focuses on work with involuntary clients in public welfare settings.

In *Working with Involuntary Clients* (Trotter 1999) I summarised a number of direct-practice skills which the research suggests are related to positive outcomes for clients in settings such as probation, child protection or mental health. These include:

1. role clarification
2. collaborative problem solving
3. pro-social modelling and re-inforcement and
4. the worker/client relationship.

The evidence-based practice model represented in this book is comprised of these four direct practice skills. The model has come to be known as the *pro-social model*—a term which provides a limited description of the integrated intervention method. (The model has four components, only one of which is pro-social modelling and re-inforcement.) Nevertheless, the term has been consistently adopted by participants in my seminars and by people who have read my earlier publications.

The model is described in some detail in my earlier book and only a summary is offered here. The concepts will, however, be further developed throughout this book.

1. Role clarification

Effective child protection workers have skills in clarifying their role. They have frequent, open and honest discussions with their clients about:

- the purpose of the intervention
- the dual role of the worker as an investigator and helper
- the clients' expectations of the worker
- the nature of the worker's authority and how it can be used
- what is negotiable and what isn't
- the limits of confidentiality.

They focus on helping the client to understand the nature of the child protection process (Department of Health 1995; Jones and Alcabes 1993; Rooney 1992; Shulman 1991; Trotter 1999).

The following example explains the notion of role clarification further. A child protection worker might put in place an ongoing method of assessing whether abuse of a child is ongoing. This might involve the worker talking to the child in private on a regular basis, a mother taking the child to a health centre on a regular basis, and the worker visiting without appointments. These things may be non-negotiable. In other words, the mother is required to comply with them. The effective worker will put time and energy into helping the mother understand what is expected and the likely consequences if these expectations are not complied with. However, the effective worker will simultaneously put time and energy into helping the mother understand that the worker also wishes to help her with any problems or issues she might be facing, particularly those problems that might have led to her abusive actions.

2. Collaborative problem solving

Effective child protection workers make use of collaborative problem-solving processes (sometimes referred to as 'working in partnership'). They help clients to identify personal, social and environmental issues that are of concern to them. In doing this they are likely to canvas a wide range of issues: finances, housing, drug use, family background, current relationships, friendships, work and schooling, health and mental health. They examine the client's situation in a broad context and they do it from the client's perspective. They then help their clients develop goals and strategies to achieve these goals (Ethier et al. 2000; Gaudin et al. 2000; Jones and Alcabes 1993; Rooney 1992; Shulman 1991; Smokowski and Wodarski 1996; Trotter 1999; and Webster Stratton 1998).

In most child protection services the child protection workers are also expected to make assessments of the risk levels of the client or client family. They are asked to gather information from the client and other sources, including relatives, doctors, school-teachers and police, with a view to classifying the client family as high, medium or low risk. They consider factors such as the nature and severity of the abuse; children's individual physical, social and intellectual development; parental drug use or mental illness; parents' acknowledgment of the problem, attentiveness to children's needs, knowledge about child development, and so on. Effective child protection workers help the client to understand this process and how it interacts with the helping or problem-solving process. Effective workers are able to assess risk and, at the same time, begin to work through a problem-solving process with their clients. They are able to integrate the risk assessment and problem-solving process.

Effective workers are able to involve their clients in case planning processes (Farmer 1999). They develop case plans which have realistic goals and are based on consensus between the professionals and the clients. Effective workers also make use of case management and advocacy skills. Where appropriate, workers refer their clients to services that will help to achieve their goals and address their problems. The workers then follow up those referrals to ensure their clients' needs are met (Fortune 1992; Gaudin et al. 2000; Rothman 1991).

3. Pro-social modelling and re-inforcement

A number of child protection studies have commented on the limitations of a partnership approach (Ammermann 1998; Gough 1993; Rooney 1992; Swenson and Hanson 1998; Triseliotis et al. 1998; Trotter 1999). Janet Stanley and Chris Goddard (1997, 2002) argue that child protection workers may effectively become hostages within family situations when they begin to accept the abuser's view. Rather than collaborating with the abusing parent to deal with the problems of abuse, the child protection worker may advertently minimise the abuse and become an ally of the abusing parent.

Collaborative problem solving or partnership approaches, therefore, need to be balanced by a third group of skills involving a focus on clients' positive and pro-social actions and comments and the use of appropriate confrontation.

Effective workers identify and reward the pro-social comments and actions of their clients. For example, they praise comments by parents which acknowledge the harm child abuse can cause. They would praise, for example, an attempt by a parent to use appropriate, non-physical means of discipline, or an attempt by a young person to reduce drug use. The more effective workers also model the behaviours they are seeking from their clients.

Again this approach is dealt with in some detail in *Working with Involuntary Clients* (Trotter 1999), where some common criticisms of the pro-social approach are dealt with, in particular, that it can be superficial, manipulative and judgmental. Suffice to say at this stage the evidence clearly suggests the approach can be influential in helping clients to change their behaviour. For this reason it is an important skill in child protection work.

4. Worker/client relationship

The fourth group of skills which the research suggests is related to positive outcomes includes relationship skills, in particular skills such as empathy, self-disclosure, humour and optimism (Department of Health 1995; Shulman 1991; Trotter 1999). When child protection workers understand their clients' point of view, when they make appropriate use of self-disclosure, when they make appropriate use of humour and when they are optimistic about the potential of the client to change, they tend to have good relationships with their clients. In turn the good relationships may lead to improved outcomes, particularly if the worker also makes use of the other practice skills referred to above.

Risk assessment

I referred earlier to the place of risk assessment in child protection services. There are some situations when children must be removed from families for their own protection, and some situations when the immediate protection of children is necessary. Making these decisions involves thorough assessment.

Much has been written about risk assessment in child protection. One child abuse computer database refers to more than 800 books and articles on the subject. There are many risk assessment profiles which require workers to work through a checklist of factors (see Holder and Salovitz [2001] for examples of risk assessment criteria).

The focus of this book, however, is not on which risk-assessment profile works best. It is on how risk-assessment processes, and the ongoing monitoring of the risk of further abuse, can be integrated with problem-solving and helping approaches.

Cultural issues

Cultural issues are often central to work with abused children and their families. David Gough and Margaret Lynch (2002) commented in a recent edition of *Child Abuse Review*, an edition devoted entirely to the issue of culture and child protection, that culture is 'the backdrop against which all circumstances and events affecting child protection occur'. They go on to discuss diversity within cultures and between cultures. Belief systems, child-rearing practices and ways of communicating vary between different groups within cultures and between cultures. Sometimes what is acceptable in one culture is illegal in another; female circumcision (or female genital mutilation) is one example.

The issue of culture is highlighted by the over representation of minority groups in child protection in many parts of the world. Indigenous populations, in particular, are over represented.

The intervention model presented in this book highlights the importance of working with clients' definitions of problems and with clients' goals. It also highlights the importance of child protection workers thinking about which values should be challenged and which values should be accepted. The intervention model is I believe consistent with culturally sensitive practice. (See, for example, John Karamoa and colleagues [2002] for a discussion about culturally sensitive ways of dealing with varying child rearing practices.)

Other models and approaches

Strengths based, narrative, solution focused, motivational and structural approaches are popular in academic circles and in many child protection and child welfare agencies around the world. It is obviously difficult to do justice to a description of these approaches in a few lines. But how do these approaches relate to the evidence-based model presented in this book?

In brief, strengths based work involves focusing on clients' strengths rather than their deficits. It is based on the belief that people learn more and progress better if their workers resist focusing on pathology and instead focus on the things their clients do well and on their achievements. It is based on the belief that even the most problem-saturated person has inner resources that can help her or him develop (Saleebey 2001).

Numerous therapeutic approaches are based on the notion of client strengths. Strengths based work is, for example, a key part of solution-focused counselling. Solution-focused counselling offers particular techniques for focusing on strengths. For example, it asks workers to focus on times when the problem was not present, to search for exceptions to the rule. It refers to the notion of 'if it works do it more', and it encourages clients to picture the way things could be, rather than the way they are (Baker and Steiner 1995).

Strengths based work is also a key part of narrative therapy which focuses on helping clients to re-author their unhelpful life stories into more productive and strengths based life stories (White and Epston 1989).

The evidence-based intervention model outlined in this book has much in common with these strengths based approaches. Pro-social modelling and re-inforcement, for example, is a strengths based approach. The focus here, however, is on pro-social strengths, or strengths which will contribute to dealing with child protection issues. Problem solving has much in common with narrative work in as much as problem solving involves examining clients' 'real' stories from the client's perspective and it involves helping the client to see different possibilities—although it differs from narrative approaches in that it encourages a focus on risk-related issues or problems and uses a specific structure to work through problems.

Motivational interviewing, even though it has been used predominantly as a therapeutic approach to address addictive behaviours, also has much in common with the model presented in this book. Motivational interviewing, like the pro-social approach, focuses on understanding the client's point of view, developing goals, accepting the client's autonomy, working with the client's definition of the problem and simultaneously persuading the client towards change. It also makes use of the notion of building confidence that change is possible and of differential re-inforcement of client comments. It varies from the pro-social approach, however, as it is less specifically targeted towards statutory clients, it is less likely to focus on situations where there are major differences in the goals of the client and the worker, and it focuses more on fostering motivation rather than developing intervention strategies (Hohman 1998; Moyers and Rollnick 2002).

The child protection literature often focuses on structural issues. For example, Parton and O'Byrne (2000) point to the socially constructed nature of child abuse. It is argued that system change is necessary to effect any real improvements for children and young people who are abused and neglected. I also mentioned earlier that there is some evidence that overall child protection services do little to alleviate the problem of child abuse (Gough 1993). There seems little doubt that poor education systems, inequality of opportunity, poor housing, unemployment, poverty, homelessness and other social problems contribute to the problem of child abuse. This book is, however, not about structural change, it is about how individual child protection workers can work within the current system to improve the lot of their clients.

It is acknowledged that the child protection worker is only one player in the child protection system. Teachers, doctors, nurses, family support workers, probation officers, friends, neighbours, relatives and many others may also play important roles. The focus of the book is, however, on how child protection workers can help the children and families with whom they work. And there is evidence in the pages of the book to suggest that, despite the structural difficulties that child protection clients face, and despite the fact that they are only one player in a larger system, individual workers can often help. They can often make a real difference.

Aims and structure of this book

This book has several aims. First, it aims to briefly outline a practice model for work in child protection, a model which was developed in my earlier book, *Working with Involuntary Clients* (1999). Second, it aims to further develop the practice model by presenting findings from a study I have recently undertaken in child protection. Third, the book aims to present in some detail what child protection workers actually do and say in their work with clients—it provides some examples of word-for-word conversations conducted by more effective and less effective workers and considers why some conversations seem to be more effective than others. Fourth, in presenting the findings from the study and the client worker conversations, I am hoping to shed more light on some of the difficult questions that are often asked by child protection workers: How do you reconcile the dual roles as helper and investigator? How do you work with the client's view of the problem when the client's view seems to be distorted? How do you focus on positives when the client's behaviour is anti-social and destructive? How do you use confrontation, humour or self-disclosure? Finally, the book aims to help readers understand more about evidence-based practice and about how to be an evidence-based practitioner.

The book is directed towards child protection workers who wish to develop their skills. In seminars I have undertaken in recent years in Europe, Asia and Australia workers often say they commonly use the practice skills referred to earlier in this chapter. Yet when they attempt role plays of those skills they often have great difficulty. I have also observed interviews conducted by experienced child protection workers who have, like Margaret earlier, difficulty putting these skills into practice. I hope the book will help child protection workers to reflect on their practice and learn from the evidence which is presented and from the examples of their colleagues.

The book will also be of interest to professionals who work with abused children and their families in voluntary agencies. While the focus of the book is on child protection workers many of the skills apply equally to work with child protection clients in other settings.

The book will be of interest to staff supervisors and trainers in child protection and child welfare. It will help them understand more about the nature of effective practice and the skills which should be developed by the workers they supervise and train.

It will also be of interest to managers and policy makers who are interested in gaining a glimpse of how things work in the field and who are interested in developing more effective child protection services.

The book will also be of interest to students and human services workers who are interested in evidence-based practice and in how they can use research evidence to develop their practice. I hope the book makes a general contribution to the literature on 'what works' in human services interventions.

This book develops the ideas presented in my earlier book, *Working with Involuntary Clients* (1999). It is different to the earlier book, however, because it focuses on child protection and child welfare and it uses material from a particular study undertaken in child protection. It also provides some detail about how effective child protection practice actually happens.

I have tried to write the book in a way which is accessible to anyone who works with abused children and their families or who might have an interest in the topic. While the book is based on a research study, I have not presented the detailed results or statistical tests. These details are available in other publications (e.g. Trotter 2002) or from the author.

Chapter 2 discusses how evidence-based practitioners can go about gathering the evidence about what works. It then outlines the study on which this book is based. It provides details about the organisation, the child protection workers, the clients, the questions which workers and clients were asked and the outcome measures. It discusses the purpose and limitations of the study. I have tried to present this material in a way which is user friendly, however, I realise that some readers will not be interested in the research methodology. If this applies to you I suggest that you skip over it and continue with chapter 3.

Chapter 3 discusses the role of the worker and how the role, as a helper or investigator, for example, relates to the outcome measures used in the study. The outcome measures include client satisfaction, worker estimates of clients' progress, case closure and removal of children from their families.

Chapter 4 examines how workers deal with their clients' problems.

Chapter 5 considers how workers help their clients to make use of other services.

Chapter 6 examines pro-social modelling and re-inforcement and how they are used in practice by child protection workers.

Chapter 7 examines the relationship between the worker and the client, particularly how the workers use humour, self disclosure and confrontation. It also considers the role of optimism and expectation.

Chapter 8 comments on the relationship between the workers' satisfaction with the work and the outcome measures, it addresses the role of supervision in effective practice and it reaches some conclusions about what works and what doesn't.

At times the book is critical of current child protection practice. I have tried however to be even handed and to focus on the positives of child protection work as well as the shortcomings.

Having worked for many years as a child protection worker I hope the book represents an acknowledgment of the invaluable work done by child protection workers. David Pelzer, a child protection client who suffered severe abuse and spent many years in the care of a child protection service in the United States, including five foster placements, commented in his book, *The Lost Boy*,

> I am forever grateful to 'the system' that so many in society ridicule without mercy . . . Very few people truly know what Child Protection Service workers go through. (1997, pp. 311–12)

I hope this notion underlies the pages of this book.

GATHERING THE EVIDENCE

In chapter 1 I argued in favour of evidence-based practice, however, I also suggested that gathering the knowledge about what works and what doesn't may not be so easy. Medical practitioners might be accustomed to consulting research articles or computer programs to get information about the efficacy of particular treatments. They might readily turn to electronic databases to search for the most effective treatment for a particular problem. It is not so straight-forward for a worker in child welfare or child protection. Information about the most effective treatment for relationship problems or poor parenting skills is not so readily available. Nevertheless, the research suggests that some approaches do work better than others and it is important the evidence-based practitioner is up to date with the research about what works.

How can you find out what works and what doesn't?

Evidence or knowledge about good practice may come from many sources, for example, from international and local journals, books, seminars and conferences and from practice experience. Some evidence, however, is more reliable and more valuable than other evidence. The most valuable form of evidence is often found in refereed international journals, such as *Child Abuse Review* or *Child Abuse and Neglect*. The fact that the evidence for a particular way of working is found in international refereed journals suggests it is likely to be sound, because these journals only publish articles which have been read and critiqued by at least two anonymous reviewers. If the methodology is unsound the article will usually be rejected.

Books are also another excellent source of evidence about good practice. Most books published by reputable publishing companies will also have a system of reviewers and generally will not be published unless they have considerable academic merit. Books may include reviews of the evidence-based literature, for example, David Gough's (1993) *Child Abuse Interventions: A Review of the Research Literature*, the British government Department of Health (1995) publication *Child Protection: Messages From Research* or Anthony Maluccio and his colleagues' (2000) book on *Child Welfare Outcome Research in the United Kingdom, United States and Australia*.

In other cases, books report on particular studies. They may contain a short literature review and provide detailed results from one study, rather than concentrating on a detailed review of many studies. By providing more detail about a particular study they can give the reader insight into the specific details of good practice. As I mentioned earlier, Laurence Shulman's (1991) book, *Interactional Social Work Practice*, was written some time ago but it continues to provide a good example. Rather than simply outlining general principles he is able to present some of the actual words that the effective workers used.

Workers can also learn about effective practice through attending seminars and conferences. In fact, often the most up-to-date information about research is available at conferences. Conferences can also be a venue for hearing unsubstantiated opinion and the evidence-based practitioner needs to be careful to examine the sources of the material presented. Some conference presentations would not meet the standards required of reputable journals.

Workers can also develop their knowledge of evidence-based

practice through the information they gather from their clients. The evidence-based practitioner is likely to ask his or her clients about whether or not the services those clients have received have been helpful or unhelpful and how they can be made more helpful. The workers will, of course, be cautious about how this information is used because it is difficult to generalise from a small number of cases and because the worker may not use a systematic method of gathering information. Further, the clients' view of what is helpful is also only one outcome measure. Nevertheless, the evidence-based practitioner over time will begin to develop an understanding of what seems to work best in particular situations. This can then be married with the evidence from the other sources referred to above.

The evidence-based practitioner is able to gather evidence from articles, from books, from conferences and from seminars, and from his or her own practice. This builds on the workers' undergraduate or post-graduate education, which should provide information about effective practice in the human services, about how to gather information about what works and about the differences between sound and unsound research. The evidence-based practitioner can then use the knowledge about what works in day-to-day work with clients.

Problems faced when gathering information

What approach should the worker take to books and articles which present new ideas or ways of working but are not yet researched. For example, the early work on solution focused and narrative work (e.g. DeShazer 1988; White and Epston 1989) developed new practice models that were not evidence based. Should the evidence-based practitioner wait until these approaches have been subjected to rigorous research before using them, even though it might take a decade for sufficient research to accumulate?

There have been many examples of intervention methods in human services that have been popular but have ultimately proved to be unsuccessful—psychodynamic groups for young offenders

(Andrews 2001; Wood 1978) and programs based on fear of punishment (Andrews 2001) provide two examples. No matter how popular or appealing a new intervention model may be, it is not possible to know whether it works until some research has been carried out. For this reason I would argue that evidence-based practitioners should be cautious about using new models until the evidence for their effectiveness is available. Not to do so is to risk doing more harm than good.

Another problem workers may face in gathering information about what works relates to the articles and books themselves. Despite the reviewing processes, books and articles might contain unsupported generalisations or they might be based on studies with poor methodology. The evidence-based practitioner needs some knowledge of research methodolgy and the ability to discriminate between a sound study and a shoddy one. Hopefully, as I mentioned earlier, the worker's professional education will have provided some knowledge about research. Certainly, critical ability is likely to be helpful in the development of an evidence-based approach.

The evidence-based practitioner may face yet another problem—time. I recommend the evidence-based practitioner make a habit of critically reading books and articles about child abuse and child welfare, however, many conscientious and hard-working child protection workers will find they simply do not have the time to do this. At the end of a busy day the last thing you might feel like doing is sitting down to read child abuse articles or learning about research methodology.

Unfortunately, the benefits which come from evidence-based work cannot be achieved without some endeavour on the part of workers, or some input from the management of child protection services. I would argue that effective child protection services need managers and workers who accept the notion of evidence-based practice. The more effective services will provide incentives for workers to read books and articles, they will maintain up-to-date libraries, they will sponsor staff to attend conferences and seminars and also allow time for ongoing training and higher education. Armed with the evidence, the evidence-based practitioner can attempt to work in a way which is consistent with the research about what works.

The child protection study

Much of the remainder of this book focuses on a child protection research study. The study confirms some of what we already know about what works, or at least adds weight to some emerging principles of effective practice. It also provides considerable detail about the precise nature of what works and what doesn't, particularly through the comments made by workers and clients and through the presentation of transcripts of child protection interviews.

I believe the methodology of the study is sound. It should be of interest to the reader that it was jointly funded by the Australian Research Council and the Victorian Department of Human Services. The Australian Research Council provides competitive funding to university researchers based on independent reviews of research proposals. A report on the study has also been published in *Child Abuse Review*, one of the most respected child abuse journals in the world. In fact, the editors of the journal refer to the study as an 'excellent example of how research can inform practice' (Gough and Lynch 2002b: ii). From the point of view of the evidence-based practitioner this is a good start. Outlined below is a summary of the context, aims and methodology of the study.

The study began when the Director of Child Protection in the state of Victoria asked if I would help her develop more effective practices among child protection workers. She was familiar with the work I had done in probation, which suggested the skills of the probation officer could lead to reductions in re-offending rates of as much as 50 per cent (Trotter 1990, 1996). She felt the skills of child protection workers could have just as much impact on the clients and client families in child protection. The managers and staff in the Eastern Region of the Child Protection Service were keen to be involved. The aim of the study was to examine what child protection workers do with their clients and how this relates to outcomes for those clients.

The Eastern Region Child Protection Service

The Eastern Region Child Protection Service is similar to many other child protection services in English-speaking countries. Services are provided to children, young people and families at all stages of the child protection process, from initial reporting to state care. The region contains both rural and metropolitan areas and a range of socio-economic and cultural groupings.

The region has about 60 child protection workers. They work in teams—an intake team which makes initial assessments; a short-term team which works with children and families for up to three months; and long-term and adolescent teams which work with children, families and young people over a longer period. The child protection teams have six to eight child protection workers and each team has a senior child protection worker, who has responsibility for staff supervision, and a team leader who oversees the work of the team.

Some of the children and adolescents, particularly those in the adolescent and long-term teams, are on court orders. The orders range from guardianship orders, under which children have often been removed from their families, to less intrusive orders, such as supervision orders which require families be supervised by a child protection worker.

The child protection workers have similar pressures to those experienced by child protection workers in other places. Victoria has experienced a doubling of notifications of child abuse during the past decade (Department of Human Services 2000) and the workers are under pressure to keep up with ever increasing workloads. The pressures are exacerbated by the need to make detailed risk assessments, to prepare reports for courts and case planning meetings, to appear in court, to involve the whole family in decision making and so on. And they do this with the knowledge that at any given time they can be held to account for decisions by an unforgiving media and an unforgiving bureaucracy. Perhaps because of these working conditions and the general pressures of child protection work Victoria's services have, like other child protection services, experienced a problem with staff turnover among the child protection workers. Many leave their positions after only a few months.

How was the study carried out?

Research officers interviewed 50 child protection workers, 282 clients and observed 13 interviews between clients and workers. The interviews were done mostly by one research officer, Jan Mumford. Jan had worked as a child protection worker for several years prior to beginning work on this project. Over a period of almost two years she interviewed most of the 50 child protection workers and the 282 clients. She also observed the 13 worker/client interviews. Most of the interviews and all the observations were carried out in the clients' homes.

On some occasions Jan did the client interviews with other research officers because we felt there might be some bias in the way she gathered the material. In each instance, however, because the interview questionnaires were pretty much self scored, it made no difference whether they were scored by Jan or the second interviewer.

Another reason for doing joint interviews on occasions related to our concern that there may have been some risk involved in interviewing clients in their homes. Jan and the other research officers sometimes found themselves wandering around a few unsavoury places and they could never be sure who might answer the doorbell. Nevertheless, the research officers said they did not feel at risk on the visits. To the contrary, the clients who were interviewed were generally very happy to talk about their experiences with child protection. Given the research about violence towards social workers (Rey 1996; Stanley and Goddard 2002) this is perhaps surprising. Or perhaps it simply reflects the notion that people are unlikely to be violent when they are not threatened.

The child protection workers

Fifty of the 60 child protection workers in the region were interviewed. Some workers could not be interviewed because they had left the region or were on extended leave when the research officer was ready to interview them. The research officers asked them a wide range of questions. The questions and the client responses are discussed in some detail in later chapters.

The workers were relatively inexperienced. Their average age was 30 years. Forty-eight per cent had completed studies in social work or welfare with the remainder, for the most part, having university degrees in psychology or other social sciences. Most had undertaken in-service training in various aspects of the work and most had undertaken training in the practice skills referred to in the introduction—role clarification, problem solving, pro-social modelling and relationships. Most were therefore familiar with the pro-social/problem-solving terminology, which made it easier to comment on how they used the various skills in their work.

The clients

The 282 clients who were interviewed were selected from the families most recently allocated to the 50 workers. The aim of the client interviews was to gather further information about the way the worker conducted interviews from the client's perspective. For example: Did the worker focus on the client's problems as the client perceived them, or on specific child protection issues? Did the worker listen? Did the worker make his or her expectations clear?

Jan initially experienced some problems with the client interviews. She spent many hours chasing clients and would often visit a client's home for a pre-arranged appointment only to find no one was home. Or she made appointments to see clients in the office and the clients did not turn up. After six months or so we decided to offer the clients a small payment (A$10.00) for each interview and the response improved substantially. In fact, almost twice as many interviews were conducted in the second year compared to the first year of the study—largely, it seems, because of the payment. Ultimately a little over half of those who were initially identified for interview were interviewed.

We aimed to interview at least one client from each family although in some cases more than one client per family was interviewed. Those interviewed included 50 adolescents (subjects of the child protection intervention), 112 mothers, 69 fathers (including de facto or common law partners), 37 other relatives, 2 siblings and 12 others (e.g. carers, friends).

The clients were from a range of ethnic backgrounds but in only 11 per cent of cases did the researcher feel the clients' difficulties with English or their cultural norms were in some way related to the child protection issues. The research officer indicated an apparent intellectual disability in five per cent of cases and an apparent psychiatric disability in six per cent of cases.

Often children or young people were referred to child protection for more than one reason. The most common reason for the referral was because those children or young people were defined as emotionally traumatised (56 per cent). Physical harm was one of the reasons given in 35 per cent of cases, failure to ensure safety was noted in 27 per cent of cases, environmental neglect in 12 per cent of cases and sexual abuse in 10 per cent of cases.

Observations of interviews

The research officer observed 13 interviews between workers and clients. We anticipated that these interviews would provide specific information about how the skills are used in practice. The observations all took place in the family home, nine of them with mothers, two with grandparents, one with a father and one with a young person and her family. In some cases children were also present but were too young to participate in the interview. The research officer wrote a word-for-word transcript of the interviews and some of this material is presented in later chapters. Similarly the research officer recorded many of the anecdotal comments made by workers and clients.

We had intended to observe more than 13 interviews, however, there was some resistance by workers to being observed. Later in the study the research officer would approach the clients rather than the workers and attempt to find out when the next appointment was to take place. The research officer would then ask the client if she could attend and she would then contact the worker. Even this proved futile in many instances.

Definition of client

In child protection work, the way in which the client is defined is important. In fact it has been argued that defining abusive parents as clients can lead to inappropriate interventions which help the abusers rather than the abused (Stanley and Goddard 2002). Child protection work is about protecting children or young people and it can be argued, therefore, that the client is the child or the young person. On the other hand, there are many occasions when the best way to help a child is by working with a mother or a father or others directly involved in the life of that child.

As I mentioned earlier, I have accepted a broad definition of client as: any family member, carer or friend who receives services from child protection. The clients are distinguished from professionals, such as child protection workers, welfare workers in other agencies, paid foster-care workers, schoolteachers or doctors.

In order to distinguish between clients who are family members or carers, and children and young people who are neglected or abused, however, I have used the term primary clients. Primary clients are children or young people who are the subject of the child protection application. For ethical and practical reasons primary clients were only interviewed if they were over the age of 12 years.

Outcome measures

This study is about what workers do and say and how this relates to outcomes for their clients. In the introduction I argued that, while outcome measures can often be interpreted in different ways, child protection interventions are likely to be better if workers and clients say they are good and if apparently concrete indications of progress such as case closure or maintaining children in their families confirm the workers' and clients' views. The interventions are not so good if these measures are equivocal or contradictory. They are worse if workers and clients say they are bad and this is confirmed by concrete measures, such as cases remaining open for extended periods and children being removed from their families.

I also argued in chapter 1 that it is better to use multiple outcome measures. In this study I have therefore used multiple outcome measures, including clients' views, workers' views, case closure and removal of children. More specifically the outcome measures include:

How would you rate the progress of the family overall?
We asked each of the workers to rate each of the client families on a 1 to 7-point scale in response to this question. The responses to this question were consistent with other questions we asked the workers. When the workers said the family was progressing well overall, they also consistently said the client and the family were progressing well in relation to the presenting problem and in terms of further risk of abuse, and progressing well in relation to any new problems which might have emerged.

How satisfied have you been with child protection's involvement in the life of your family in terms of the outcome?
We asked the 282 clients to rate their answers to this question on a scale of 1 to 7. The client outcome measures, like the worker outcome measures, correlated closely with each other. When the clients were satisfied with the outcome they were also satisfied

with the way things happened and with the primary worker. They were also likely to say they would contact the worker again in the future if they had problems.

Has the case been closed?

This information was gathered from the case files, on average, 16 months after the interview with the worker. If the case was closed this is viewed as a positive outcome measure. The official reason for closing cases in child protection in Victoria is that the family is no longer at risk.

Has a child or young person been placed away from his or her family in a department of human services facility (e.g. foster care)?

Again, this information was gathered from the case files about 16 months after the interview with the worker. Keeping families together is a common objective in child protection and is viewed as a positive outcome. Schene (1995), for example, found that reducing or minimising child placement was mentioned as an objective in many United States child protection services. It is also one of the objectives of the Victorian service.

We gathered other information from the files. We considered further notifications during the period of supervision and after case closure, however, this measure proved to be problematic because when children and families remained under supervision they tended not to be re-notified. If further incidents of abuse occurred a report would often be made directly to the child protection worker rather than a new notification being registered. Further notifications were therefore more likely to occur if cases were closed early.

We also gathered data on critical incidents. For example: Did children die or parents or young people overdose on drugs or attempt suicide? Nineteen critical incidents were recorded on the files. Despite the seriousness of these incidents, however, the numbers of them were too small to provide any statistically meaningful information about effectiveness.

Criticisms of the outcome measures

As I mentioned in chapter 1, outcome measures like these can be criticised. A particular criticism of the client satisfaction outcome measure could relate to the definition of the client. As I discussed earlier I am using a broad definition of client to include mothers, fathers, carers, grandparents and so on. A good outcome for a primary client might, however, be a poor outcome for a parent. For example, the study suggests that young people who are placed away from their parents usually see this as a good outcome, whereas the parents tend to see it as a poor outcome. On the whole, however, the ratings of the 50 young people in the study correlated strongly with the ratings of other family members, even though the young people tended to rate their satisfaction more highly. Nevertheless I have referred to instances when the primary clients or particular client groups (e.g. mothers) have expressed different views about the outcomes.

A further criticism of the outcome measures might relate to their subjectivity. Workers might base their judgments of family progress on inadequate information. They may not know what is actually going on in the family. Clients might be happy with the outcome because they are left alone. Cases might be closed because of high workloads, and children are often removed because it is necessary for their protection. Each of the measures, however, tended to correlate with the other measures. In other words, when workers reported good progress, clients reported satisfaction with the outcomes, the cases were more likely to have been closed and children less likely to have been removed. This suggests they are meaningful outcome measures.

On the other hand, it could be that these measures correlate with each other as a result of what David Gough and Margaret Lynch (2002b: ii) refer to as 'a process of joint socialisation between client and worker'. In other words, when workers believe the clients are progressing well in terms of the presenting problem, this in turn leads those clients to feel the outcomes are positive, which leads to workers closing cases earlier and to children remaining with their families.

Could this process occur even though abuse is continuing? This seems unlikely for several reasons. Removal of children and, to a lesser extent, case closure, are for the most part decisions made in consultation with more senior staff. In fact, in many cases decisions to remove children are made by courts rather than the child protection service. Further, the clients in this study were often not the perpetrators of the abuse—they were sometimes grandparents, other carers or persons in the extended family. These people would have been less likely than the immediate family to have been involved in a 'socialisation process' with the worker. There is also evidence in my earlier study in community corrections (Trotter 1996) that there is a significant correlation between client views of their progress and the hard data measure of further offending. The clients seemed to know when they were doing well.

The outcome measures used in this study can therefore be criticised. They do contain a degree of subjectivity. Nevertheless, these measures are often used in child protection research (Gaudin et al. 2000; Schene 1995; Shulman 1991). For the reasons outlined above, I believe they are meaningful measures. They can tell us a lot about what works and what doesn't.

Risk levels and statistical significance

This book is about the relationship between the skills of workers and the outcomes for their clients. Those outcomes may, however, be related to the risk levels of the clients. It is likely that the lower-risk clients would have better outcomes than higher-risk clients. Therefore in determining the effectiveness of any intervention we need to take account of risk levels.

Child protection workers in the eastern region undertake a risk assessment on all new cases. This involves the worker collecting information from the client, the client's family, from schools, doctors, police and any other relevant sources, and making an assessment of the severity of the child abuse and the extent to which it is likely to be repeated. The workers then categorise the family as of no further risk, moderate risk, significant risk or severe risk. The risk assessment process proved very successful in predicting case closure and removal of children—four times as many high-risk families remained under supervision after 16 months compared to low-risk families, and children were removed in 25 per cent of high-risk families but in none of the low-risk families. The risk assessments are therefore used in the study to examine whether the results are related to the risk levels of the clients.

A relationship between the worker's use of particular skills and client outcomes can occur simply by chance. I have used a number of statistical tests to examine the likelihood that the various results are simply chance occurrences. The results reported in the chapters that follow are those unlikely to have occurred by chance and are independent of the risk levels of the clients. (More detail on the statistical tests is available in the *Child Abuse Review* article [Trotter 2002] or from the author.)

Drawing conclusions from the outcome measures

Developing and testing general principles for effective child protection practice raises a number of issues. At what stage can we say a general principle is supported? For example, we may wish to consider whether reaching agreement on specific goals between the worker and the client relates to better outcomes. First we would need to determine whether the worker and the client have reached agreement on specific goals. But what if the client says she or he reached agreement on specific goals but the worker does not agree?

We then need to determine whether the outcomes are good or not so good. What about when the client is satisfied with the outcome but the worker feels the client has not progressed? Or

what if the children have not been placed away from their families but the case has stayed open longer than other cases?

If the relationships are in the expected direction we might have different requirements than if we see unexpected relationships. For example, if we were looking at the relationship between reaching agreement on goals and the outcome measures, a positive relationship with one outcome measure may be sufficient to persuade us the relationship is a meaningful one (assuming there are no negative relationships with the other outcome measures). On the other hand, if a relationship with the outcome measures was in an unexpected direction we would want to see this relationship with more than one of the outcome measures. So if we found a positive and significant relationship between not reaching agreement on goals and the client satisfaction with the outcome we would look to the other outcome measures before we reached any conclusions.

Sorting out these issues presents a challenge to the researcher and in turn to the evidence-based practitioner. They are judgment issues and there are no right or wrong answers. I have taken the view in this book that a particular worker skill as described by either the client or the worker is an effective or valuable skill if it is in the expected direction, and if it is significantly and positively related to one or more of the outcome measures (and not negatively related to any of the outcome measures). If it is positively and significantly related to two, three or four of the measures it can be considered more effective.

If, however, a particular skill is more effective in this study does it mean it will be more effective in another place and another time? For example, if setting goals is related to positive outcomes in this study does it necessarily mean that setting goals will be related to positive outcomes in a child protection service at another time and in another country?

The extent to which the results of research can be generalised from one population to another is open to debate. The issue is discussed further in the final chapter, however, the skills which appear to be effective for workers and clients in this study are the very skills which have been seen to be effective in many other studies. They are the skills which numerous research studies in a range of different settings have found to be effective (Trotter 1990, 1996, 1999). This research has predominantly been undertaken in English-speaking countries, nevertheless it suggests the skills of effective practice tend to be similar across a range of countries and settings. It seems we can learn a lot from each other wherever we come from.

The qualitative research

The following chapters report many of the comments which clients and workers made in the interviews with the research officer. Excerpts from some of the worker/client interviews which were observed by the research officer are also included.

With the assistance of the research staff we used a qualitative data analysis program to examine more than 100 000 words of transcript. The data analysis program enabled the text to be broken down and grouped into themes. Qualitative research of this nature tends to be exploratory and to develop themes rather than reach definite conclusions, however, it does provide some valuable illustrations of how different skills are used in practice.

I have introduced each of the chapters with quotes from the more 'successful' child protection workers. These are the workers who reported their clients were progressing well and who also had clients who were satisfied with the outcome of the child protection intervention.

Summary

This chapter lays down the background of a study undertaken in an Australian child protection service. The study includes interviews with workers and clients, observations of interviews and data from files about placement of children and case closure. The aim is to examine the relationship between what child protection workers do, and how this relates to outcomes for their clients. The difficulties relating to the definition of the client is acknowledged, as is the difficulty in defining outcome measures. The study uses a broad definition of 'client' and multiple outcome measures.

CHILD PROTECTION WORKERS—HELPERS OR INVESTIGATORS?

> I try to work at the client's level. I try to engage the client so we have a working relationship and I also try to give good information and establish boundaries. I talk about why we are involved, how we can work together to deal with the problems. I avoid using a militant approach. I try to work on their motivation rather than the motivation which derives from a court order.
>
> Comment by a 'successful' child protection worker.

Child protection services in English-speaking countries have become overly forensic and investigatory. In chapter 1, I referred to several commentators who expressed this view. I also referred to some research which suggests the primary focus of many child protection services is on risk assessment at the expense of helping, treatment or problem solving. It is often argued in turn that abused children would be better protected if there were a greater focus on helping or a more balanced approach which embraced both investigatory and helping roles (e.g. Parton and Byrne 2000).

What is meant by an investigatory approach? Let's take the example from the introduction, Mr Pope who has physically abused his daughter Sophie. If the worker, Margaret, adopted a forensic or investigatory approach she might involve the police in her initial visit to the family. She would then focus on risk assessment. Her agency would probably expect her to use a risk assessment framework which will involve gathering as much information as possible about Mr Pope and Sophie: information about the severity of the injuries sustained by Sophie and how and why they occurred; whether or not there was any history of abuse by Mr Pope; whether Mr Pope had a history of violence, substance abuse or mental illness; the extent to which his expectations of Sophie are reasonable and his level of knowledge about child development; the extent to which he accepts responsibility for the abuse which has occurred; the level of care he otherwise gives to Sophie; and whether Mr Pope has any support in his care of Sophie.

Margaret would talk to other professionals who know about the situation and probably talk again to the person who referred the case to child protection. She would make an assessment of Sophie's development, keeping in mind the expected stages of development of a child of her age. She would be interested in any behaviour problems which Sophie might exhibit, such as persistent crying or soiling.

Margaret would come to a conclusion about whether or not the report of abuse was substantiated and make a recommendation to her supervisor regarding the level of risk of the family. In some child protection systems the case might be allocated to a long-term worker. Margaret or the new worker might then proceed to court with a recommendation that the family be placed on a supervision order. She would develop a case plan which might require Mr Pope to comply with certain conditions in order to keep Sophie at home with him. These conditions might include a visit on a daily basis from a nurse or a requirement for him to take Sophie on a regular basis to a community health centre. It might involve the worker visiting several times a week in the initial stages and checking that Sophie has no new bruising. It might involve a family support worker spending 10 or 15 hours per week with Mr Pope and Sophie.

Margaret would keep in touch with the health centre, visiting nurse and family support worker, as part of an ongoing monitoring program relating to the degree of risk Sophie faces. The case plan might also involve Mr Pope being directed to attend a parenting skills group or an anger management group. Margaret would be very clear about what was required from Mr Pope and the consequences of not complying—perhaps increased supervision or a return to court.

What on the other hand is meant by a helping role? If Margaret were to adopt a helping role she would focus on the issues facing Mr Pope in his parenting role. She would try to identify the issues of concern to him. Does he have problems with housing, with loneliness, with money or with illegal drug use? She would then try to develop a case plan that would help Mr Pope to address these problems. She would focus on the problems as Mr Pope defines them. She would also focus on Mr Pope's strengths rather than his deficits. She would encourage him to care for his daughter as a single father rather than focus on the abuse. She would also, with the agreement of Mr Pope, make appropriate referrals to specialist services.

Coming back to our study, are the child protection workers overly forensic or investigatory? Or do they focus more on helping their clients? Or are they both helpers and investigators? If they see themselves as investigators, does this lead to poorer outcomes for their clients? If they see themselves as helpers, do their clients have better outcomes? I argued in the introduction that the more successful child protection workers are likely to adopt a dual role and put some energy into helping their clients to understand the nature of the workers' role. In other words, they talk to their clients about their role. Did this occur in our study? These questions are examined in this chapter. The answers have implications for child protection workers, for training, for staff selection and for the shape of child protection services.

The clients' and the workers' views about these issues are presented below along with some of their more anecdotal or qualitative comments. Some excerpts from the worker/client interviews are also presented.

Are the study's child protection workers overly forensic?

In the view of the clients their workers were not overly forensic. We asked the clients to select from a number of words the best description of their worker. The term most frequently chosen by the clients was 'helper and supporter' (see Table 1)—although they also often selected the terms investigator and case manager.

Table 1 Clients' description of their workers

Helper/supporter	36%
Investigator	32%
Case manager	32%
Problem solver	27%
Friend	21%
Adviser	21%
Mediator	20%
Counsellor	18%
Referral agent	15%
Supervisor	11%
Police officer	8%
Adversary	8%

The primary clients, young people over the age of 12, were most likely to identify their worker as a helper, or as a friend, counsellor, mediator or adviser. In fact 38 per cent of the adolescents described their worker as their friend. This again suggests many clients do not view the child protection workers as forensic or investigatory. The other relatives were also more likely to identify their workers as helpers rather than investigators. The mothers and fathers, on the other hand, were slightly more likely to identify the workers as investigators rather than helpers.

The clients in this study do not support a view that child protection workers are overly forensic. What about the workers?

We asked the workers to rate themselves on a 1 to 7 scale with investigator at one end and helper/supporter at the other. The mean rating by the workers was 4.32. In other words, they were slightly more likely to see themselves as helpers rather than investigators.

We also asked the workers a number of questions about how they did their work. Again, this supported a view of the child protection workers as having a helping as well as an investigatory role. A clear majority of workers indicated they did helping things, such as focusing on understanding the client's definition of the problem, looking for and rewarding client strengths, and helping the client to understand the purpose of the intervention. They were clear, however, that they also focused on establishing whether abuse had occurred and on confronting and challenging clients. The child protection workers clearly see themselves as embracing a dual role as both helpers and investigators.

Do the child protection workers have a balanced approach?

The clients did not see their workers as embracing a dual role. They tended to perceive their workers either as helpers or as investigators. In only 10 per cent of cases did the clients describe their workers as both helpers/supporters and investigators.

The clients' descriptions of their workers tended to either cluster around the helping or the forensic orientation. When the clients described their workers as helpers and supporters they were also inclined to describe them as problem solvers, friends, advisers and counsellors. On the other hand, when the clients described their workers as investigators they often also described them as case managers, supervisors and referral agents.

The views of the workers and the clients differ on the extent to which the workers embraced a dual role. The workers saw themselves as embracing a dual role as helpers and investigators. The clients tended to perceive their workers as either helpers or investigators.

Do helpers or investigators do better?

Did the clients do better when they felt their workers adopted a more forensic orientation or a more helping orientation? The results suggest that workers with a more helping orientation did better. When the clients described their workers as helpers and supporters 75 per cent of those clients indicated they were satisfied with the outcome of the child protection intervention compared to only 46 per cent when the clients described their workers as investigators.

Similarly, the clients were more positive about the intervention when they described their workers as friends, advisers, problem solvers and counsellors. They were least likely to be satisfied with the child protection worker or the outcomes when they described their workers as investigators, supervisors, case managers or referral agents. This was the case whether the clients were adolescents, parents or relatives.

It seems the clients often saw their workers as helpers and supporters and they often felt they were helped by workers who they described as helpers and supporters.

Do workers who adopt a dual role do better?

In the small number of cases when they identified their workers as both investigators and helpers, the clients did particularly well. When the clients saw the worker as both an investigator and helper they were much more likely to be satisfied with the outcome of the intervention (87 per cent satisfied compared to 52 per cent when not seen as having a dual role), they were significantly more likely to report the family was progressing well (77 per cent compared to 61 per cent), the children were much less likely to have been removed from their families (4 per cent compared to 11 per cent), and the cases were slightly more likely to have been closed.

These results are perhaps not surprising. Lawrence Shulman

(1991) came to precisely the same conclusion in his child protection study in Canada. He gives an example of the kind of comment the more effective workers in his study were likely to make:

> I am here because we received a call from someone who felt you might be neglecting your child. I have to investigate such calls to see if there is any truth in them. I also want to see if there is any way we might be helpful to you. (Shulman 1991: 27)

This theme was also very clear in an earlier study I did in corrections (Trotter 1996, 1999). The more effective probation officers made it clear to their clients they wanted to help as well as being clear about what must be done to comply with the probation order. Getting the balance right between social control and helping seems to be a very important skill in work with involuntary clients.

The worker's role as described by the workers

When we talked to the child protection workers about their role much of what they said supported the views expressed by the clients. The outcomes were better when the workers said they adopted a helping role. The more they described themselves as helpers rather than investigators the more positive they were about the progress of the families.

We asked the child protection workers to comment on their knowledge base, including a range of approaches or theories, which they use in their work. The workers most frequently referred to child development theory (92 per cent) and risk assessment frameworks (92 per cent). Others commonly identified included counselling and listening skills (80 per cent), case planning principles (80 per cent), case management principles (80 per cent), systems theory (68 per cent) and cognitive behavioural theories (68 per cent).

Only two of these factors related significantly to any of the outcome measures. When workers identified counselling and listening skills, the workers were more likely to rate the progress of the client family highly. When they identified risk assessment frameworks they were more likely to rate the progress of the family poorly.

The workers, unlike the clients, tended to see themselves as both helpers and supporters rather than as one or the other—although when they indicated they embraced a dual role with their clients they did no better on the outcome measures.

Client risk levels

Low-risk, short-term clients tended to perceive their workers more as investigators than as helpers. Long-term, high-risk clients, on the other hand, were more likely to describe their workers as helpers, friends and advisers. This trend is even more evident when the very high-risk group of clients are considered.

I mentioned earlier it is sometimes argued that, while a helping role may be appropriate for most children and young people who enter the child protection system, a small proportion, maybe ten per cent, require a more forensic response. I referred to the words of David Thorpe:

> There are children who are the victims of serious neglect, phys-ical or sexual assaults. They require protection and approximately ten per cent of children drawn into the mouth of the child protec-tion net will filter down into this category. The use of emotive words such as abuse, maltreatment and perpetrator, should be confined to those cases. (Thorpe 1994: 202)

This argument suggests the focus should be more on helping low-risk clients and more on investigating and monitoring high-risk clients, particularly very high-risk clients. It does not appear from our study, however, that the very high-risk families were receiving a more forensic response and the lower-risk families a more helping response. In fact, the results point to precisely the opposite situation.

Of the 282 clients interviewed 20 were identified as coming from severe high-risk families. Sixty per cent of these clients identified their workers as helpers and supporters. Only 15 per cent identified their workers as investigators. In other words, the severe high-risk clients were twice as likely to identify their workers as helpers and half as likely to identify them as investigators, in comparison to other clients.

It is not hard to understand why workers might tend to adopt a helping relationship with severe high-risk families. These families are usually longer-term clients of child protection and known well to their workers. Over time friendly and supportive relationships often develop between workers and clients. Or it might be, as Janet Stanley and Chris Goddard (2002) argue, that the stress and trauma associated with child protection work can lead workers into denial in relation to the presence or severity of further abuse. This, in turn, they argue can lead to a reluctance to maintain an investigatory focus.

These are the families who it could be argued should be receiving a forensic response. They are the victims of serious neglect, or physical and sexual assaults. This is evidenced by the fact that in 25 per cent of these cases children were removed and placed in departmental facilities. Yet these clients feel they are receiving a helping rather than an investigatory service.

Should we be critical of this? The view that high-risk families require a forensic response might be quite wrong. It may be that the high-risk families need help and support a lot more than they need investigation. The clients themselves seem to have this view. When the clients from severe high-risk families described their workers as helpers they were positive about the outcomes—58 per cent reported they were satisfied with the outcome, compared to 37 per cent who were satisfied with the outcome when the worker was not identified as a helper supporter.

The clients who perceived their workers as helpers did not, however, do better on the other outcome measures—worker estimates of client progress, time to case closure or children being placed away from home. Nevertheless, the results provided some support to the arguments being made more recently that attempting to stream child protection clients into forensic or helping services based on their risk levels is a simplified solution to a complex issue (e.g. Hetherington 1999).

This study certainly supports the argument that in general terms the workers who do best are those who are able to combine the investigatory and helping roles and the workers who seem to do worst are those who have a predominantly investigatory focus. This seems to be regardless of the levels of risk of the clients.

Workers' attempts to clarify their role

A number of research studies suggest that outcomes for child protection families and for other involuntary clients are better if the worker spends time helping the client to understand the nature of the worker's role (Andrews et al. 1979; Jones and Alcabes 1993; Shulman 1991; Trotter 1999; Videka Sherman 1988). Jones and Alcabes argue that the client does not in fact become a client until he or she understands the nature of the worker/client relationship and accepts that the worker can help.

I anticipated, therefore, that when workers talked a lot about role-related issues their clients would have a better understanding of these issues and the clients would in turn have better outcomes. (By role-related issues I mean issues such as: how the worker can be both helper and investigator, the worker's authority and how it might be used, negotiable and non-negotiable areas, the purpose of the intervention, the client's expectations and confidentiality.)

The child protection workers in our study had only limited discussion with their clients about their role. While the clients tended to describe their workers as helpers it seemed that they developed this view from the way the worker interacted with them and from the things the workers did, rather than as a result of specific discussions about the nature of the helping role. When we asked the clients to rate the extent to which the workers talked about their role as helpers the average rating was 1.4 on a 7-point scale. In other words, they hardly talked about it at all. Similarly the workers talked very little about their authority and how they might use it (1.37 on the 7-point scale).

The clients felt the workers were more inclined to make use of other role clarification skills. For example, they were more inclined, in the view of the clients, to discuss what was negotiable and what was not negotiable. The rating on this question was 4.5. The clients also indicated that their workers often discussed other aspects of their role, such as the purpose of the intervention, clarifying expectations and confidentiality (rating 4.7).

Workers' attempts to clarify their role and the outcomes

While the clients indicated that discussion about the worker's role as a helper occurred infrequently, when it did occur the clients were more than twice as likely to be satisfied with the outcomes of the child protection intervention. Similarly, despite the infrequency of discussions about the workers' authority, the clients were more satisfied with the outcomes when they indicated their workers talked about authority. The question we asked the clients was: 'Has your worker discussed with you issues relating to how he or she might use authority, for example, in what circumstances would the worker recommend taking action in the children's court or recommend removal of a child?'

While the clients were not positive about the workers they saw as taking a less helping and more forensic or case management role, they were positive about workers who were clear about their authority. This is reinforced by the responses to the question: 'Has your worker spoken to you about what was negotiable and what was not negotiable, in other words, what things had to stop or change, what things you (the client) could decide whether or not you wished to change?' When the clients responded positively to this question they were more positive about the outcomes (67 per cent compared to 45 per cent when the worker did not talk about what was negotiable).

Another aspect of the workers' role which we thought would be important relates to the way the worker clarified and discussed issues, such as the purpose of the intervention, the clients' expectations and confidentiality. When the clients indicated that their workers discussed these issues they again reported more satisfaction with the outcomes.

The picture continues to emerge of the more effective child protection workers talking about their role, particularly their role as both a helper and an investigator.

The workers' views about their use of role clarification skills

Most of the discussion so far in this chapter has focused on the clients' views about the workers. When we asked the workers about the importance of making use of the role clarification skills the same trend was evident. When the workers indicated they talked to their clients about the helping role, the workers rated the clients' progress higher. The clients progressed even better if the workers indicated the family members responded to the discussions about the workers' role.

There is some difficulty in interpreting these results. Clients are more positive about the outcomes when they feel their workers talk to them and help them understand the nature of the child protection worker's role. Workers are more positive about the outcomes when they say they focus on helping clients to understand the nature of the role. However, the positive results are only there with some of the outcome measures. In no instances are role clarification skills related to poor outcomes. On balance it seems fair to conclude that role clarification skills are valuable and in many cases related to better outcomes.

Client comments

The comments below from workers and clients and the excerpts from the interviews which follow shed some light on the practicalities of role clarification—about what the more effective workers say and do to help clients understand their role. The comments were made by clients who provided a high rating for the outcome of the child protection intervention and who the workers believe made good progress. In other words, they are the clients who were doing well in their own estimation and in the view of their worker. The clients often focused on the friendliness of the worker:

> She is very nice and would have been a friend if she was not so busy.

> She was quite friendly, she was fantastic, always there when I needed her.

> She comes across as friendly and caring even though she is a worker and I realise she would not be likely to come for coffees with me if she wasn't working.

> It was like she enjoyed seeing us as a family. She helped me a lot.

Other clients focused on the clarity of the worker in terms of his or her dual role as helper and investigator. One mother commented, 'She is a person who makes me aware. If I don't look after the children properly she will take action, such as taking the children away—which I need. I feel comfortable talking with her, she smiles.'

The clients who felt they had poor outcomes were more prolific in their comments and their comments had a familiar theme. Some were concerned about the worker's lack of interest in them. One adolescent boy who was most unhappy with his worker and with the outcome was unclear about who the worker was supposed to be helping:

> The worker has nothing to do with me. She doesn't talk with me. She doesn't consult with me. When I ring up I get brushed off.

I don't know the woman after all this time. She's nice and caring, but listens to my mother and not me.

One grandfather felt that the worker did not have a role in helping him:

There was nothing positive in her role. She never wanted anything positive for me. She was working with the father who recently came back into the child's life after a three-year absence.

Another mother was concerned about the worker who she felt '. . . was a helper and supporter of the child but not to me'. And another mother did not see the worker as having a helping role: 'She's not available to help me. She never gets back to me. She doesn't follow through with getting help.'

Others were concerned about the lack of honesty and openness on the part of the worker. One mother commented:

After the notification, at first I allowed the worker to interview me and the children twice for two hours each session. Then I got the court report regarding the older child with its distortions and untruths; so when they tried to allocate a new children's worker and she wanted to interview me again I refused all contact. I was not going to leave myself open for my name to be dragged through the mud again.

Another mother whose son had been removed said, 'I say things like, my son has called around and then they send the police to check if my son is staying here, which proves he [the worker] doesn't know and trust me, which wrecks the relationship.' And another said:

They say they're there for the child—but they kept changing their stories and I didn't know what to think. I was told first that reports had been made, but was not clear about when or how many times—the story kept changing. It was too confusing. Also the story changed on how many children were involved. She was always taking notes when I did not know she was.

A number of clients were also concerned that the work was of no practical help. A mother commented:

> She's not available to help me. She never gets back to me. She doesn't follow through with getting help. For the child they probably do the best but not for me. They let the child do what she wants to do. They let her get away with murder.

A grandmother commented:

> Their mother recently overdosed in front of the child at my house and the department did not see that as a problem. I could not believe that they did not react. Yet when the child was a baby and her mother knocked a chair over they made a big deal of it. Anyway when the overdose happened we had no worker at the time. The previous one had left and no new worker had been allocated. We had to be told to ring the supervisor if there were problems but when we tried to ring to tell them about the overdose nobody cared; they didn't see it as a crisis.

What client comments tell us about good practice

The notion of the effective worker as a friend, as someone who actually enjoys the contact with the family, who the client can feel comfortable with, who smiles and is interested in the client, comes through strongly in the client's comments. I mentioned earlier that 38 per cent of the adolescents in this study described their worker as a friend. More clients saw their worker as a friend than as a supervisor or counsellor. This is not an isolated finding. In my earlier study in adult probation almost 50 per cent of the offenders on probation and parole described their worker as their friend. They were also more satisfied with their supervision when they described their worker as a friend and they reoffended less often, even after taking account of client risk levels (Trotter 1993).

Yet the clients' perception of the workers as their friends seems to represent a misunderstanding of the role. The clients are clearly not the workers' friends in the generally accepted meaning of the term. Further, misunderstandings relating to this issue can be problematic. Anyone who has worked in the helping professions will have experienced clients who misunderstand the nature of the professional relationship and seek an inappropriate friendship with their workers. Yet when clients see their workers as friends they seem to do better. This may represent a reflection of the social isolation of many clients in the child protection system. They may perceive a friendly person as a friend because they do not have more conventional experiences of friendship.

On the other hand, the clients with poor outcomes in this study tended to focus on the worker's lack of honesty and lack of interest in them. They were often concerned about whose side the worker was on.

It could be, of course, that the clients who do well have friendly interactions with their workers simply because they are doing well. In other words, the good outcomes lead to good interactions, and poor outcomes lead to unfriendly interactions. Which comes first, the poor outcomes or the unfriendly interaction? It is hard to answer this question. All we can say is that there is an association between the outcomes and a friendly, interested demeanour. The more effective workers were also clear about their authority, which helps their clients to understand the limitations of the relationship.

Worker comments

The following comments were made by workers whose clients were satisfied with the outcomes of the child protection intervention and who felt that their clients were progressing well. They could be considered 'successful' child protection workers.

I talk about where this can lead, what can happen, what are the differences between our role as child protection workers and the role of workers from other agencies. And I talk about the notes I am taking and what they can be used for.

My understanding of role clarification is that it is about presenting your role in a non-threatening way, especially in relation to the possibility of having to go to court. It is about coming back to your role throughout the interview, about being open to the client, about being willing to handle the client's anxiety and allay his or her fears.

It involves talking about the nature of the intervention, what are the parameters. Are they clear?

It is about clarifying responsibility, the limitations—what workers can and can't do. It is about helping the clients to understand that the child is always the client but working with the parent to help with parenting is to help the client.

It is about what we do with the information, about discussing conditions of the order and what they mean, about letting them know their rights, legally. And it is about acknowledging and talking about their fear of the department.

Who you are, why you are there; and how information will be used.

There was a different flavour to the comments made by workers who were negative about the progress of their clients and whose clients were negative about the outcomes. The following two examples suggest a narrow view of the role of the child protection worker:

In role clarification the emphasis is on explaining the court process and how to avoid it.

It is about explaining the mandate in a more user-friendly way, about being clear and using language they understand. Some information may not be correct, so we are there to explain it.

What worker comments tell us about good practice

The workers who did well with their clients commented less about friendliness than their clients, and more about purpose and boundaries. They indicated that they focused on the role of the child protection worker and the role of other workers—what could happen or where the intervention might lead, the anxieties or fears of the client and what the worker can or can't do. One of the more successful workers also referred to explaining the purpose of file notes. The few comments by the workers who did not do so well with their clients suggest they tend to focus on the mandate and the court process.

Worker/client interviews

As mentioned before, the research officer observed 13 worker/client interviews and wrote word-for-word transcripts as she went. Perhaps the most interesting factor to come out of the data analysis of the 13 interviews was how little the workers made use of role clarification principles. This is consistent with the clients' comments, which suggested the workers rarely talk about their dual role as a helper/investigator or about how they use their authority.

Having spent many years teaching students about the importance of helping clients to understand the role of the worker I anticipated that the worker/client interviews would focus on these issues. I expected they would begin with summaries of purpose and there would be frequent references to issues of confidentiality, what the client expected from the intervention, what was negotiable and what wasn't, as well as some discussions about the workers' dual role.

I particularly expected to see these skills displayed in the interviews because the workers who agreed to do interviews were a select group.

We only managed 13 interviews out of the 50 we planned at the start of the project largely because of the resistance of the staff. It seems likely then that those who volunteered were good staff members with good skills. They were also probably concerned to display their skills given that they were being observed. The results confirmed that they tended to be good workers—their clients tended to have better outcomes than other clients on the client satisfaction measure and on the worker progress measure.

There was, however, very little discussion in the interviews about role clarification. Less than three per cent of the discussions in the interviews we observed could be described as focusing on role clarification. There was no discussion at all in any interview about the dual role of the worker as helper and investigator, confidentiality, the use of authority or clarifying the clients' expectations. Less than 2 per cent of the discussions focused on what was negotiable and what was not negotiable. And less than 1 per cent focused on talking about the purpose of the intervention or the interview. The interviews were generally conducted with longer-term clients, well known to the workers, and it may be that some of the role-related issues had been discussed in earlier interviews. Nevertheless, given that role clarification is usually seen as an ongoing practice skill, it seems surprising that it received so little attention in these interviews.

The following case examples provide two of the few instances where there was some discussion about role clarification. In the first example the client and the worker were reasonably positive about the outcome and the progress of the family. In the second they were negative. The first example is from the case study referred to in the introduction.

Shortly after Brent and his wife Bridgit broke up, Bridgit began using drugs heavily. Child protection removed the children and placed them in temporary foster care. Child protection then placed them with Brent. This interview took place more than one year later.

Brent told the research officer that he had a high opinion of the child protection worker. He had been working with her for more than a year and he has found her friendly, open, fair and a good supervisor. He also believes, however, that the child protection worker did little to keep the mother and the children together and that if things had been handled differently ('more support and less attack') the children might still have an ongoing relationship with their mother. On the other hand, he is happy the children are now progressing well in his care.

The worker, Maria, is about 30 years old and has worked in child protection for only two years. She is very happy with the progress of this family and very positive about Brent. She believes the children have progressed very well and the outcome for the family has been good. In this excerpt from the interview in Brent's home the worker talks to Brent about the need for a further court order to ensure that the children can stay with him.

Worker: We need to talk about foster care payments. The order lapses in a few weeks and we need an annual review.

Brent: The payment stops then?

Worker: Yes, we need a meeting. We need to get on to this because it is possible that she (the mother) could get interim orders in the Family Court.

Brent: What would that entail?

Worker: We need to get you an interim residency—it's just a holding order so the kids can legally stay with you. I'm not an expert in family court matters.

Brent: I'm not expert on adoption but I know the things I've come up against before.

Worker: It is difficult—with different things going to the family court and the children's court. Last year when we extended custody, did a solicitor come to see the kids?

Brent: No.

Worker: Oh, yes, they would have been too young. Now it's just a matter of the solicitor coming so an independent person can hear what the kids want. Anyway we need an annual review meeting. One possibility—I could apply to the Children's Court to extend the order to the hearing date, and in that time your solicitor would be able to get interim residency in the family court. I am not sure I'm explaining this properly.

Brent: What you're saying is if we get an interim thing in the Children's Court that gives time to get a Family Court order.

Worker: It takes time to get a Family Court order.

Brent: What happens with this scenario—you have to try to contact Bridgit? What if she came and wanted them back?

Worker: You're safe—there is a departmental recommendation and the Family Court can subpoena our file. We would say you were a suitable carer and that there are concerns with Bridgit. In the Children's Court we have to give parents the opportunity to show they can care for their children. The Family Court is different. In the Children's Court we try to return kids to parents if possible. In the Family Court it's past this stage.

Brent: It was already past that when she didn't do the rehab.

Worker: She hasn't contacted the kids since she left?

Brent: Once or twice in the first couple of weeks but that's all. Last contact with James was two years ago.

Worker: If the last contact with their mother was nearly two years ago I don't think you have anything to be concerned about.

In this discussion the worker is helping the client to understand the legal situation and the negotiable and non-negotiable areas. She also refers to her own lack of expertise in this area and the role of the solicitor in the process. While the interaction is a positive one, it is focused very much on practical issues. And it is hard to say how much the worker is actually engaging with what Brent says. The outcomes for this family were generally positive, but ultimately Brent feels the intervention has been unsatisfactory because the children have lost their mother. The focus on practical rather than feeling issues may be more comfortable for both worker and client in these circumstances.

In the second case example there is also some discussion about what is negotiable and what is not negotiable and a brief comment about the purpose of the interview.

Serena has three children aged 7, 9 and 11. She was a victim of domestic violence over a period of several years. At the time of the initial notification the child protection worker classified the risk of physical injury to Serena and her children as very severe. Since this time the children have been taken to court and placed in the care of the department, and their father has been charged with assault and imprisoned for a period of six months.

When Serena was interviewed some months after the initial notification she spoke very negatively about the child protection worker. She rated her satisfaction with the outcome at 1. She described the worker as an investigator, adversary and a police person. She also indicated that her worker had not talked about having a role to 'help and support her and her family', although she had talked about what was negotiable and what was not negotiable. Five weeks earlier when she was interviewed the worker was more positive about the overall progress of the family, rating it at 4 on the 7-point scale.

At the interview is the mother, Serena, her new partner, Jack, and the worker. Serena is pregnant to Jack.

> Worker: The reason we are here today is to talk more to you [addressing Jack] rather than Serena. Serena has asked for you to go to access with her. This has been previously refused, because we weren't sure how long you'd be here—it can be very hard on the kids to introduce partners. But now you're having a baby, you obviously have some commitment to the family—so we want to look at you being there for access. We need, however, first to do a police check—the police check their records and give information to us. The department is only interested in issues of safety for the children—protecting them from violence. If there were any problems we would discuss them with you. We want your signature, your written permission, so there is no misunderstanding.
> Serena: Do your check—it's alright, it should be basically okay.

Worker hands the pen to Jack. Jack signs. The pen has been left in the sun and is bent.

> Serena: Looks like an ergonomic pen. Who's doing access?

Worker: I understand you and Serena are wanting to take the kids to the movies.

Jack: Can we go swimming instead?

Worker: Not if you are also going to the movies. The access is only for two hours. Do you want to go swimming instead of going to the pictures?

Jack: No.

Worker: The way it was negotiated was two hours at the movies at Southland. This has been arranged with Kylie, the family support worker. She will be meeting you there.

Jack: I have signed this [handing back the form].

Serena: When you get it back will you give me a call? It will only have driving offences—and he had a gun once.

Jack: And there was a fire hydrant.

Worker: Do you mean you took a fire hydrant?

Jack: I took it to use it as a chair and the police charged me because they reckoned it wasn't my property.

Discussion ensues about a range of matters, including some discussion about the need for exercising after the birth of a child.

Serena: Do you have children?

Worker: I don't talk about that as I'm employed not as a parent but as a social worker. Any other questions?

Serena: It is just that I wanted to talk about access between the three children.

Worker: They will see each other every Saturday and Sunday for the next three weeks. It is not clear if you would be going every week?

Serena: It doesn't matter what you say anyway, it is up to the department, isn't it?

Worker: Michele (Serena's daughter) is not keen on seeing you anyway—it is not personal.

In this discussion a number of comments by the worker are not consistent with the principles of good role clarification. The comment, for example, that the 'department is only interested in issues of safety for the children' suggests the department (and presumably the worker) may not be interested in helping the family members with their problems. The comment that Michele was not keen on seeing her mother could have been rephrased to be less confronting. For example, 'Michele is still feeling confused about what has happened and feels let down. Maybe at some stage I can help you with your relationship with her.'

The response to the question about the worker's children is also problematic and seems to lead to a more negative interaction with the client immediately afterwards.

Lawrence Shulman (1991) in his Canadian child protection study suggests that the more successful child protection workers would be on the lookout for opportunities to help clients understand the workers' role. He suggests that in responding to the question, Do you have children? the more successful workers would look to the meaning behind this question. Is the client concerned about the worker's ability to understand what it is like for him or her? Does the client feel that some sharing of personal information is reasonable given the highly personal information which child protection workers have access to? Or is the client simply questioning the worker's credibility? He suggests an appropriate response might be, 'I don't have children. Why do you ask? Are you concerned about my being able to understand what it is like for you raising three kids? I'm concerned about that as well. If I'm to help you, I will need to understand. Can you tell me what it is like?' (Shulman 1991: 45)

Summary

Much of the recent literature suggests that child protection services are too investigatory or forensic. This study does not support this view. In fact, both workers and clients were slightly more inclined to view the child protection workers' role as helping rather than investigatory. The clients tended to view their workers as either helpers or investigators rather than as both helpers and investigators, however, the child protection workers who did best were those who were perceived by their clients as both helpers and investigators and those who did worst were seen by their clients only as investigators. One very stark finding was that workers who indicated they made use of counselling and listening skills reported positive progress among their clients, whereas workers who focused on risk assessment frameworks reported negative progress.

Another very stark finding was that workers seemed to talk little about their role with clients, particularly their dual role as helper and investigator. In fact, in about 12 hours of worker/client interviews we could not find one example. The clients, unlike the workers, also indicated that such discussions rarely occurred. It seems that workers put little energy into one of the key aspects of effective practice—helping their clients to understand the dual role of the child protection worker. Nevertheless, when they did talk about their role their clients had better outcomes.

Another interesting finding was that high-risk clients are much more likely to view their workers as helpers and low-risk clients more likely to view them as investigators. This presents another dimension to the forensic/helping debate. Child protection workers may be excessively focused on risk assessment and investigation with low-risk, short-term clients, but may pay too little attention to risk factors when working on a long-term basis with high-risk families. Maybe this provides some explanation for the high-profile child protection 'failures' which seem to keep happening despite the attention of child protection and other professional workers.

What are the implications of these findings for child protection workers? Generally speaking, workers should focus more on coming to terms with their dual role as helper and investigator and on helping their clients understand the nature of this role. Workers should talk to clients more about the role of the worker. Workers should also be careful not to adopt a purely investigatory focus.

4

DEALING WITH CLIENT PROBLEMS

> It is about identifying what the client sees as problems—discussing and negotiating. About the worker being very open and looking broadly at issues—exploring and broadening the picture. Once you have agreed on the problems it's about setting goals and prioritising tasks, including other people and setting time frames—and being concerned about evaluation.
>
> Comment by a successful child protection worker.

In chapter 1, I referred to literature which suggests that work with involuntary clients is likely to be effective if the worker has an understanding of the issues or problems of concern to the client and reaches agreement with the client about what the client wishes to achieve and how to go about achieving it. This notion is sometimes referred to as working in partnership. It involves the key elements of problem-solving processes—identify the problem, set goals, then develop strategies to achieve the goals. There is also some evidence that work with involuntary clients will be particularly effective if the worker and the client focus on the issues that have caused the client to become a client—in other words, the risk-related issues, such as drug use, anger or family relationships (Andrews et al. 1979; Trotter 1996; Trotter 1999).

Were the child protection workers in our study doing these things? Did the clients do better when their workers did these things? These questions are the focus of this chapter. Before considering these questions however it is interesting to look at some of the criticisms of problem solving. In recent times there has been some criticism of problem solving, despite the fact that it continues to be a core part of many social work and helping texts (e.g. Hepworth et al. 2002). In particular problem solving is questioned by supporters of solution-focused approaches, which promote a focus on goals and solutions rather than problems (e.g. Baker and Steiner 1995; DeJong and Miller 1996; DeShazer 1988) and supporters of strengths based approaches which recommend focusing on client strengths or things that clients do well, rather than focusing on client deficits (Saleebey 2001).

Outlined below are some of the reasons I have chosen to use a problem-solving framework to analyse the work of the child protection workers in this study. First—it works.

The research on the effectiveness of work with involuntary clients suggests problem-solving approaches are effective. In other words, the problem-solving model presented in this book is an evidence-based model. It has been developed out of the evidence about what works. The research outlined below suggests that specifically defining problems from the client's perspective and then developing goals and strategies to address the problems is consistently related to improved outcomes.

In 1973, Joel Fischer published an article called, 'Is Casework Effective?' (Fischer 1973). He suggested casework does not work—that welfare clients who receive casework services are no more likely to have better outcomes than clients who do not receive casework services. Other reviews of casework services in the 1970s came to similar conclusions (e.g. Wood 1978). Fischer (1981), however, revised his view some years later. He expressed the view that casework works sometimes. It does not work when it relies on psychoanalytic- and insight-oriented approaches and it does work when it focuses on more structured approaches involving clear definitions of problems, the development of methods to address those problems and the use of contracts.

In the 1980s, a plethora of studies emerged which pointed to the effectiveness of problem-solving approaches, including clear definitions of problems, exploration of problems and the setting of goals (Reid and Hanrahan 1981; Rubin 1985; Sheldon 1987). To quote the Rubin (1985: 474) review:

> These forms of practice (problem solving) were found to be successful with such diverse groups as mildly to moderately retarded adults, chronic schizophrenics in after care, young non-chronic psychiatric inpatients, women in public assistance and low-income children experiencing school problems.

To quote the Sheldon (1987: 572–3) review: '[more effective approaches involved] clearer and more concrete definitions of problems', and 'a more thorough assessment of problems prior to intervention'.

More recent research on task-centred practice, a problem-solving model developed over the past three decades by William Reid and others, has pointed again to its effectiveness with a wide range of client groups. Reid (1997) cites more than 30 published studies pointing to the effectiveness of the model. He quotes the conclusion from one of the studies: 'The greater degree of focus on the target problem, measured by the amount of time spent on it, was associated with problem change' (Reid 1997: 135).

Reviews of the effectiveness of interventions in child welfare have also supported the value of specifically defining client problems. A review of effective interventions in child protection by Shulman, for example, cites a number of studies to support the proposition that, 'helping clients to manage feelings and to manage problems [results in] a positive working relationship with clients' (1991: 291). He argues that 'moving too quickly to solutions . . . before adequate exploration of issues of acceptance and motivation may well result in leaving the client behind' (1991: 113). His research suggests that the skill of helping clients to manage problems is related to the trust developed by clients in their worker and, in turn, to hard outcome measures, such as the number of days children spend away from their families and the frequency of court appearances. A later review of the effectiveness of child welfare services by Smokowski and Wodarski concluded that 'problems must be prioritised' for intervention to be effective (1996: 519).

The second response to the arguments against problem solving is that strengths based practices can be readily integrated with problem solving. In fact, many of the authors who write about problem solving (e.g. Compton and Galaway 1999; Hepworth, Rooney and Larson 2002; Reid 1992; Trotter 1999) argue strongly for the incorporation of strengths based approaches.

There is also some research evidence which suggests that workers can successfully integrate both strengths based practices and problem solving. My study in corrections, for example, found a clear relationship between the use of problem solving by probation officers and the re-inforcement of positives in their clients (Trotter 1996). Those officers who identified and explored problems also focused on client strengths by re-inforcing pro-social behaviours and comments. The issue of integrating strengths based work with problem-solving approaches is addressed further in chapter 6.

Problems for clients and problems for workers

Problem solving is therefore an evidence-based approach. How did the workers in our study use problem solving and how did it work? The clients we interviewed had many problems. On average the clients identified seven different problems they were facing. These problems ranged from family relationships to drugs to social isolation. The term 'multi-problem families' certainly applies to this group. The clients most commonly identified problems with family relationships (64 per cent), stress (62 per cent), children's out-of-control behaviour (42 per cent), anger management (42 per cent) and finances (35 per cent).

For the most part the problems identified by the different client groups were similar. For example, primary clients, mothers, fathers, carers and other relatives all identified family relationships as the most common problem. In some cases, however, the different client groups expressed different views. The primary clients, for example, were less likely to be concerned about finances, but more likely to be concerned about domestic violence and physical harm. Parents were more likely to be concerned about stress and out-of-control children. Other relatives were more likely to be concerned about parenting skills, lack of supervision and emotional harm.

The workers consistently identified fewer client problems than the clients themselves. For example, 62 per cent of the clients identified stress as a problem, whereas only 11 per cent of the workers saw this as problem for their clients. Sixty-four per cent of clients identified family relationships as a problem but only 42 per cent of the workers identified this issue as a problem. And 35 per cent of the clients saw finances as a problem, compared to 11 per cent of the workers.

When the workers did identify client problems they also tended to identify different problems to the clients. While, like the clients, they identified family relationships as the most common problem (42 per cent), other problems they commonly identified included parenting skills (25 per cent), drug and alcohol use (20 per cent), emotional harm to children (19 per cent) and domestic violence (13 per cent).

Not only did the workers tend to minimise their clients' problems, they also conveyed their views to their clients. Generally, the clients felt their workers underestimated the number of problems they were facing, particularly problems with finances and stress.

Were problems reduced under child protection supervision?

Even though the clients felt their workers underestimated their problems, more than 90 per cent of the clients reported that at least some of their problems had been reduced since they began work with child protection. Many clients felt these problems had resolved themselves through their own efforts or through changes in circumstances, however, more than 40 per cent felt their worker had contributed to the problem reduction and that the outcome would have been worse if the worker had not been involved.

A smaller proportion (31 per cent) of clients felt that at least some of their problems had got worse since they began work with child protection. Most attributed this to circumstances or to their particular situation; for example, a deterioration in finances or a deterioration in family dynamics. In only 25 per cent of cases, where the clients had felt their problems had got worse, did they attribute this to their worker.

These figures are consistent with a lot of research about the impact of social services interventions, which suggests that they can be for better or worse. Most clients are influenced in some way—some benefit from intervention, some are harmed by intervention—but overall there is a tendency for more to benefit than to be harmed (Reid 1997; Trotter 1999).

The clients were generally positive therefore about the help they received with their problems from their child protection workers. These views were generally consistent with the views of the workers, who tended to be positive about the progress of clients in terms of the presenting problem in the notification (4.7 on the 7-point scale), in relation to new problems (5.6), and in relation to the progress of the family overall (4.6).

While the workers and clients tended to feel the problems were reduced during the child protection intervention, our study does suggest, as we predicted, that some workers did better than others. One factor in how well the clients did was the problem-solving skills of the worker.

Are outcomes better if the client defines the problems?

In our study, we anticipated that clients would do better if their workers talked to them about a range of problems. We also

anticipated the clients would do better if they defined the problems rather than the worker. This was clearly the case.

When clients indicated their worker had discussed specific problems with them 71 per cent were satisfied with the outcome of the intervention compared to 34 per cent if the worker had not discussed specific problems. The workers also reported that the client families were progressing better when the problems had been discussed. Similarly, when the client indicated that he or she defined, decided on, or named the problem, the client was more than twice as likely to be satisfied with the outcome. Again the workers also reported good progress. The same positive outcomes were apparent when we asked the clients if the worker discussed 'your real problems as you define them'.

Goals

The research referred to earlier suggests that when workers and clients agree on specific goals, clients do better. We asked the clients if goals had been set in relation to their problems. About half indicated that goals had been set. When the clients felt that goals had been set, 61 per cent were satisfied with the outcome of the child protection intervention, compared to 40 per cent when goals had not been set. Similarly, when goals were set the worker reported the overall progress of the client and client family was better.

In situations where goals had been set we asked the clients to comment on who set the goals. When the clients felt they, rather than the worker, set the goals the clients were even more likely to report the outcome was positive. The cases were also more likely to have been closed after 16 months.

Tasks

We asked the clients a number of questions about whether strategies or tasks had been set with their worker to address the goals.

When tasks had been set the clients were generally more positive about the outcomes. In particular, they were more likely to believe the outcomes were positive when the tasks had been set by the clients and client family members rather than the workers. When the clients believed the workers completed the tasks that had been set, the outcomes were positive—the clients were more positive about the outcomes, the cases were more likely to have been closed and children were less likely to have been placed in departmental facilities.

This is consistent with some research, which suggests that child welfare clients appreciate workers who do practical things to help (Triseliotis et al. 1998) although to some extent it suggests a new perspective on the development of tasks and strategies. Much of the literature on problem-solving approaches (e.g. Reid 1992; Rooney 1992; Trotter 1999) refers to the clients carrying out tasks to address their problems and goals. The emphasis is on empowering the client to do things for themselves. However, these findings suggest it may be just as important for the workers to carry out tasks and strategies to assist the clients. This may have something to do with modelling appropriate behaviours (discussed in more detail in chapter 6). The worker completing tasks might also give the client a sense of partnership, which in turn leads to better outcomes.

Contracts

We asked the clients if they had contracts with the workers, either written or verbal. The research officer explained to the clients that a contract involves a written record of problems, goals and strategies (consistent with a problem-solving approach). In only 18 instances (less than 1 per cent) did the clients report that a contract had been developed with the workers. This is surprising given the prominence contracts have in much of the helping literature (e.g. Compton and Galaway 1999; Hepworth et al. 2002).

The workers agreed that they made little use of contracts, suggesting they were more inclined to focus on problem exploration and developing strategies. Given the infrequent use of contracts between workers and clients it is hard to say whether they were helpful or not—although the results do suggest the clients were more satisfied with their workers in the small number of instances when contracts were used.

Client comments

In the following examples the clients were satisfied with the outcomes of the intervention and the workers reported the family was progressing well. It is clear in each case that the workers and clients have reached at least some agreement regarding the nature of the problem. One mother commented:

> The child protection worker said that I had to find somewhere else to live or the children would be removed. But where was I to go? I'm not moving my children into a caravan park. I couldn't live with my mother. My father smokes and Zac has respiratory problems. What was I to do? I had to lie to them so I wouldn't lose my kids but I had nowhere to go. Eventually I moved in with my father for a while and then they allocated a new child protection worker and she helped me find new housing.

Another mother said:

> Anna had been living with her father but was staying with me; however, problems arose in relation to the man I was living with. I was not aware of the problem Anna had with him and she did not discuss it with me. She was initially unhappy about staying with me as she had to change schools and was looking for negatives. After the child protection worker got involved she relaxed and was much happier and she is now happy living with me.

A young woman in foster care who was happy with the outcome of the child protection intervention and whose worker felt she was progressing well said:

> My worker discusses finance, drugs, and lots of other things—checking out for problems. He doesn't often miss things, but when he does I remind him . . . finances, court, even my sex life—although that is not something he can help me with.

In another case, an aunt caring for her sister's child was very happy with the worker and the outcome. She commented:

> My task is to go to a monthly meeting at the department—to get the child involved in social programs, like sport. The worker has offered to take the child to the pictures but he won't go. We feel we should listen to what they say—they are more experienced.

In the following examples the clients were not satisfied with the outcome and were not progressing well. It is clear that workers and clients have different views about the extent and nature of the clients' problems. A father commenting on his 15-year-old daughter, who had been placed on a guardianship order, said:

> She had run away a couple of times before but she always came back. She was a pathological liar. She could never mix with children and I never thought she was quite right mentally. She was okay one minute and angry the next. I did a lot in the early years—took her to basketball and stuff, but she said I did nothing and they (child protection) believed her. Her problems are now much worse. Her behaviour is out of control now.

A mother who was most unhappy with child protection commented:

> We weren't having any problems with our daughter until she met her boyfriend. He has got an anger problem and he drives

recklessly. Anyway, she left home and when she left I was upset and tried everything to get her back. She wanted money and went to the Department of Social Security and created a story of abuse to try to justify getting living away from home allowance. Then Child Protection got involved and it was after this that the problems began, as allegations began to be made against us, her parents. Mary raised issues of sexual abuse. What actually happened is about six or seven years ago her brother and her were involved in show and tell. This had stopped after three months but the child protection blew it out of proportion. Her brother has admitted the issue and even when he wanted to talk to the child protection worker to give his side it took several days to get the worker to see him.

In the following example a mother was concerned that tasks had not been kept:

There have been no tasks set for me but the tasks for Sonny have not been kept. I don't think what they were doing was appropriate. I felt he should have been referred to a psychiatrist but he wasn't. I feel I should have had input into the planning meetings. He was supposed to meet weekly with a youth worker and another worker but they did not seem to do much else. Then they tried to get him to do training in the department but he wouldn't go.

Another dissatisfied mother said:

They told me I had to do drug screens, drug and alcohol counselling, Mum's group, but I was already going to my Mum's group. I had been going since before the baby was born, and that really annoyed me. I can find these places on my own. I don't know if there is anything she [the worker] was meant to do. She leaves me to do it.

Another mother commented:

> She doesn't see what I see as priorities, as her priorities. We have our joint goals, then I have my goals as well, which she doesn't see as a high priority. I want to play ice hockey so I can develop a social life; I also need a job—as well as controlling the children. Also I have had so much to do at once and I cannot do it all.

The father of a boy who was removed from his family and placed in a foster home was very unhappy with the outcome of the intervention, although the worker felt the overall progress of the family was reasonable. The father commented:

> I've found the worker not the most accommodating person. She is not helpful in solving problems. We have arguments. I'm trying to get my view across but there is a lack of understanding about cultural issues. We Italians speak with raised voices and waving hands and she always took a 'stand back' attitude. She showed a lack of understanding and she did not want to understand—altercation, wrangle, quarrel. I feel marginalised and estranged due to my cultural background. Their attitude is 'We have the guardian-ship—we don't have to listen to him'. They treat me like an imbecile. They never take the time to ask me to repeat or to understand what I say.

What client comments tell us about good practice

The clients' comments support the other findings in this study. The outcomes were best when the worker and the client had similar perceptions of the nature of the problem and when the workers worked with a range of client problems. The outcomes were poor when the clients felt the workers did not understand the nature of their problems, when they set inappropriate tasks, when they did not acknowledge the efforts the clients were making, when no tasks were set, and when tasks were not carried out.

Worker comments

It seems clear that when clients felt their workers understood their problems and worked through a problem-solving process those clients did better. Workers also felt they did better when they made use of problem-solving processes. When workers said they had made use of problem solving with particular families, they rated the progress of the families significantly higher; even higher if the worker indicated the family responded to problem solving. The clients were also more likely to be satisfied with the outcome.

Outlined below are some comments made by workers who had good client outcomes. In other words, the clients were satisfied with the workers in terms of the outcomes and the worker felt the clients were progressing well. The comments help to clarify the nature of the problem-solving process for these workers.

It is about looking at what the family sees as a problem and seeing where it agrees or differs with the department—it's about trying to find mutual goals.

It's about engaging clients to look at their perception of the problem—dealing with issues from the client's perspective or perceived concerns, as well as protective concerns. Working on how to plan more collaboratively—contractual decision making.

It is about articulating what the client sees as the issue, time frames, not having unrealistic expectations, and working on things the client agrees on: What are the issues? What do we need to do to solve them? Setting goals and making clear what is expected, for example, using a checklist of who is to do what.

Working together on figuring out what the problems are—getting them to point out what the problems are. Finding out from them what needs to happen to change that.

Below are some comments made by workers who had lower than average ratings on both their own estimates of the progress of client families and on the clients' satisfaction with the outcomes. In the first example, the worker has an understanding of the process, however, she does not acknowledge the need to look beyond why the department has become involved.

> Problem solving is about getting the client to identify the problem. Getting the client to say in their own words why the department has become involved.

From another worker we heard:

> I acknowledge what they want, but work more on my view of the problem.

The worker who made this comment had six clients who were interviewed for the study. Each of the clients provided low ratings in terms of their satisfaction with the worker and with the outcome of the intervention. In fact, the average rating on the client outcome measure was only 1.8 on the 7-point scale, in other words the clients were particularly dissatisfied with the outcomes.

While these comments are only a few examples of the ones made by workers, they are typical of the comments made by the more effective and less effective workers. The comments represent a reflection of the more objective ratings.

Observations of the interviews

Most of the interviews observed by the research officer were between workers and clients who had been working together for some time. This might account for the apparent lack of structure in the interviews. We had anticipated that we would see more of the specific components of problem solving, particularly given the comments by many of the workers. We thought we would see,

for example, reviews of problem lists, detailed exploration of particular problems, setting of goals, discussion of contracts, specific strategies to address goals, reviewing of progress towards particular goals, and so on.

This was not the case, however. I mentioned earlier that the research officer who undertook the qualitative data analysis read through the full transcripts of each of the interviews and entered the material into a qualitative software program. In doing so, she was unable to identify any specific examples of goal setting or the development of contracts. The discussions tended to focus on what might be described as problem exploration and identification of tasks. An excerpt from one of the interviews illustrates this.

The worker has been seeing a family for more than one year. The primary clients were Rebecca, 18 years old, Wendy 16 and Michael 12. They were judged by child protection to be at significant risk after their mother died. Following her death the three children continued to live with their father, however, he is a heavy drinker and child protection had concerns for the children. Wendy was the only family member interviewed and she said she was very happy with the worker, and with the outcomes of the child protection intervention. She rated both responses at 7 on the 7-point scale. She also indicated she would contact the worker again in the future if she had a problem. The worker was not so enthusiastic about the progress of the family, rating it at 4 on the 7-point scale.

In the following example, the child protection worker is doing an office interview with the children's aunt and uncle. (It was the aunt and uncle who made the initial report to child protection as the mother's health deteriorated.) About 15 minutes into the interview Wendy and Rebecca arrived, informing the worker that Michael was at home in bed.

Rebecca: We have been on the road since 6.30—the buses are so slow.
Worker: Yes, I know how slow they can be.

Wendy: I told her we had to be here earlier.

Worker: You called this meeting. Can you tell us your reason?

Wendy: Because me and Michael and Rebecca want to move out.

Rebecca: We were up until 11 o'clock last night working things out. [Hands over pieces of paper with budgets, etc.]

Worker: How's Dad?

Rebecca: He is sick. When he is not drinking, he seems like he is about to have a fit—he is all shaky.

Aunt: What will you do if he is put in hospital?

Rebecca: His brain is shrinking and with each fit there's a chance he'll die, but he leaves the doctors and he immediately asks us to get him two beers.

Aunt: He needs someone to be with him.

Wendy: He doesn't have fits until after he stops drinking so he wants to keep drinking.

Worker: I haven't seen Michael—he is not at school?

Rebecca: He can't go. Dad has no money. He is buying a slab or two a day. We looked at Dad's bills for three months and multiplied it by four to work out an annual budget. We will be earning $280 per week. Wendy is working at Hungry Jacks®. I will be getting student support because I am homeless. You don't have to attend full time at school to get support . . .

Wendy: I was going to school until Dad had a fit and there was no money available.

Worker: Do you know if your father is getting payments for Michael?

Aunt: Family payments.

Worker: They are only made to adults.

Rebecca: $100 a week is enough for food. We would have enough money.

Aunt: We still may be able to access the trustees. I don't know what they would hand over. Even if I still had trustee money I don't know if I could have handed it out . . .

Rebecca: I'm not asking.

Aunt: Your father would have to handle it. Unless you want to get on to them or get July [the social worker] on to it. It is out of my hands.

Worker: What about setting up costs—furniture?

Wendy: I have all the stuff for the kitchen.

Rebecca: When Mum was going to leave him he agreed to give the kitchen furniture to her. He signed a letter and the solicitor has a copy of it.

Wendy: He'd kick up a stink, so we would have to do it when he's out.

Worker: How would your father react if he came home and all the kitchen furniture was gone?

Uncle: The microwave doesn't belong to him.

Worker: Have you considered other options?

Rebecca: We have but we want to stay in our area and people will help us out. The three of us want to be together.

Worker: What are the obstacles to moving out?

Rebecca: We need a bond and a month's rent.

Uncle: How much do you need?

Rebecca: Altogether we need 500 to 700 dollars for the bond.

Worker: How will you get the money?

Rebecca: We can either save up somehow or you said you spoke to those people.

Worker: What about—the lease?

Wendy: Don't know.

Worker: About the bond? You obviously have something in mind—you always do.

Wendy: We could get you two [referring to the aunt and uncle] to sign for the lease and we could live there and pay the bills.

Worker: What are the estate agents saying?

Wendy: The only way is if someone else signs. Otherwise the owner may not agree.

Aunt: What about John? [A relative on the father's side.]

Rebecca: We don't even speak to him. None of that side will help us.

Aunt: What is the responsibility of the person who signs?

Wendy: If anything breaks it comes out of the bond money, but we will only be there to sleep and eat. We will be at school.

Uncle: If you default in the rent?

Wendy: We won't default.

Worker: What if the owners find out you are living there and not your aunt and uncle?

Rebecca: They won't. Or we'll say our parents are away.

Worker: What if there are complaints?

Rebecca: There won't be.

Worker: What about Michael?

Rebecca: People don't understand—he'd be better out. Dad's the problem.

Worker: It seems that Michael is up all night and sleeps all day.

Rebecca: He doesn't sleep all day.

Worker: What does he do?

Rebecca: He just hangs around the house.

Worker: So he hangs around with Dad? I understand it's difficult at home. I understand you've put in a lot of work and have your heads together to sort all this out—but what about Michael?

Rebecca: He'll be okay. He'll do anything to get out.

Worker: What other problems do you see?

Rebecca: None. It might be hard at first with the bills. We've told Michael if he stuffs up once he's out and in a foster home and he said fair enough and agreed straight away.

Worker: How will you handle the safety aspect—people thinking that they can stay with you when they want to?

Rebecca: They won't. We don't want complaints so we have to make it work.

Worker: So you're saying there will be no problems?

Aunt: I'd be scared.

Rebecca: It will be scary at first but it will be okay.

Worker: What about if something happens to your dad—he gets sick and there is no one with him?

Wendy: I don't care. He comes into the bathroom, he grabbed Rebecca

by the throat and punched her in the stomach. He attacked Michael—he grabbed his ankle in the street. He went at me and the cat with a knife.

The conversation continued about obstacles and planning. They went on to discuss what will happen to the dog and more about the furniture and the budget.

The strengths of this interaction are that the clients have defined the problem (their father and their need for alternative accommodation), the worker (with the help of the aunt and uncle) is working through the problems from the clients' perspective, and the clients have a clear goal (they wish to live elsewhere)—although this goal is not spelt out in specific terms. The clients have also developed a solution to the problem. Obstacles which might get in the way of the proposed solution to the problem are also examined.

The following interview took place between a child protection worker, a mother Tina and her 13-year-old daughter Sacha. The clients and the worker were less positive about the intervention than in the example above. Sacha was not very satisfied with the child protection worker. She rated her satisfaction with the child protection worker at 3 and her satisfaction with the outcome at 4 on the 7-point scale. The mother rated them slightly higher, at 5 and 5 respectively. The worker rated the overall progress of the family at 4.

Sacha is on a supervision order following several incidents of running away from home. She has been under the supervision of the worker for about two months but was previously supervised by another worker. She is now living with her mother, Tina. They are discussing a recent incident when Sacha ran away from home again.

Worker: What was the problem?

Tina: If I confront her when I don't want her to do something she gets angry. Don't you, Sacha?

Worker: Things were really good when I met you months ago and then it seems there was a rough patch.

Tina: Everyone has rough patches.

Worker: Everyone does but not to the point of saying they are going to live elsewhere.

Tina: I can't remember now why it happened.

Worker: Was it something to do with the neighbours.

Tina: That's right, the next door neighbours—Monte.

Sacha: Her mother went off her tree about caring for the guinea pig. I was supposed to be giving it water when Monte was away. Her mother kept ringing and saying the guinea pig has no water.

Tina: She is a misery, that woman. I am cross with her.

Sacha: I was supposed to be looking after the house. The car was in the drive. I went to water the plants and heard, 'fuck this' and 'fuck that', and something about my touching the car. I was just watering.

Tina: I told you, you shouldn't go there.

Sacha: Okay, okay, get over it.

Worker: There were a couple of things that you didn't do when your mother asked?

Sacha: She [referring to her mother] cracked the shits about the arguments with the neighbours.

Worker: So the argument was about you being rude.

Sacha: Mum yelled because I was rude.

Tina: No I didn't, I wasn't yelling.

Sacha: You were so. She didn't care what she [the neighbour] said and threatened. All she did was get cross because I was there after dark.

Worker: With the neighbours was the problem hanging outside late at night?

Sacha: They got prank calls and Monte's mother thought it was me.

Worker: Haven't there been problems with staying out late at night?

Tina: One night I yelled because she was still out at 10 p.m. and she blew up. Everything is fine unless I ask her to do something.

Worker: So when you were asked to come in Sacha, why didn't you come in?

Sacha: I was just sitting and talking, I wasn't doing any harm.

Tina: She thinks she should be able to stay out.

Sacha: It was Friday night.

Tina: It was happening a lot—staying out.

Worker: Is there an agreement about when Sacha is to come in?

Sacha: 9.30.

Worker: Is that every night?

Tina: It is often 11 p.m.

Sacha: Why are we talking about all this now?

Worker: We are trying to work out what went wrong so it won't happen again. The things that seem to be problems for your mother are: being rude, not coming inside, being out past the agreed time. Anything else?

Tina: No, everything's fine now. But I don't think she should be out there.

Worker: It seems fair that she has a time to be in.

Tina: Yeah, she's better now.

Worker: Sacha, what do you think led to the rough patch?

Sacha: Don't know.

Worker: A few weeks ago you said you felt upset at things your mother said—like she would ring the department and get you placed in a home?

Sacha: Once she said it three times in a week.

Tina: I tell you if you want to live here you have to be respectful.

Sacha: You use it as an excuse. You don't even know what I'm trying to say.

Tina: I'm listening—say it.

Sacha: No—you're not listening.

Worker: So it really hurts when your mother says that?

Sacha: Yeah, and she acts like it's fine, like she has said nothing.

> Worker: And when the neighbour threatened you, your mother gave you no support?
>
> Sacha: Yes, that's right.
>
> Tina: But she stayed outside even though I was telling her to come in. You disobeyed me.
>
> Sacha: All right, all right, you told me a month ago.
>
> Worker: I think at that time there were things happening with your friends—Robert and . . .
>
> The conversation continues about Sacha's friends.

In this interaction the discussion is less focused on the client's definition of the problem than in the earlier example. Sacha asks at one stage why they are talking about staying out late. The goal or purpose of the discussion is not clear, and probably because there is no clear agreement on what the problem is, there is little done in terms of developing tasks or solutions.

At one stage the worker summarises or reviews the issues facing the mother. This is consistent with a problem-solving approach, however, the worker only reviews the issues facing the mother. If she were using an evidence-based, problem-solving approach more faithfully, she would have also reviewed the issues facing Sacha.

Summary

The research on work with involuntary clients, including work in child protection, suggests that interventions are more successful if the worker focuses on the client's definitions of the problems. The clients in this study, however, tended to identify more problems than their workers believed they experienced, and in many cases they identified different problems. Nevertheless, when the clients indicated they talked about their problems with their worker the outcomes were better.

It was apparent that the workers make little use of specific role-clarification skills, such as helping the client to understand the dual role of the worker. It is also apparent they make little use of specific problem-solving skills. They discuss and explore problems with clients but they rarely appear to identify specific goals or use contracts. Nevertheless, the clients often reported their problems were reduced with the help of the worker, and when the workers did use the specific skills the clients did better.

One particularly interesting result was that the outcomes were better if the workers as well as the clients completed tasks. I suggested this might have something to do with the modelling process by the worker and this is discussed further in chapter 6.

5

WORKING WITH OTHER AGENCIES AND CASE CONFERENCES

> We'll all sit down together and look at what sorts of things you
> want. She can say what she can help you with when you meet
> her. It is better you get it from her.
>> A successful child protection worker making a referral.

C hild protection work involves working with other agencies and other professionals. The problem-solving process often involves referring clients to other agencies to receive treatment for particular problems. Workers make referrals because they may feel the clients' problems are outside their field of expertise. Alternatively, the child protection system might require that treatment for some problems be undertaken by workers in other agencies.

In some cases, the whole child protection function, including case planning and treatment, may be contracted out by the child protection service to a voluntary agency. In these instances the voluntary agency accepts full responsibility for case planning and the implementation of the case plan—although the agency may not have the power to make major case planning decisions, such as removing a child or discharging a case.

The idea of contracting out case planning and treatment services to voluntary agencies has its critics. In fact, as I write a debate is raging on the front page of the daily paper about a one-year-old child who was found dead with her mother in her flat. Her case had been contracted out to a voluntary agency and the social worker from that agency had not had contact with the child for a week. She had tried to contact the family after three days but could get no response. She then contacted child protection and four days later child protection workers forcibly entered the home with the assistance of the police. They found two dead bodies.

Journalists questioned why the social worker from the voluntary agency did not have the power to call the police and forcibly enter the home herself. They also questioned the advisability of contracting out case management in high-risk cases, such as this one.

Certainly such a situation might have been avoided if the child had been under the direct supervision of a child protection worker or if the voluntary agency had the full child protection function, including full legal authority—a situation which occurs in some European child protection services (Heatherington et al. 1997).

The rights and wrongs of the structure of child protection services are not the subject of this book—it is about effective practice. Part of effective practice is, however, working with other agencies and other workers in order to ensure the needs of clients and families are met. Effective practice also involves bringing together family members and workers from other agencies in decision-making and planning processes, such as case conferences. These subjects are the focus of this chapter.

Working with other agencies

In many cases child protection workers maintain case planning responsibility for their clients but much of the direct therapeutic work with those clients is undertaken by specialist workers, usually employed by voluntary agencies or non government authorities.

In other words, child protection families continue to be supervised by child protection workers but are referred for specialist assistance from such places as family support agencies or drug treatment agencies. Those agencies then work with the clients and client families on their particular problems. The child protection worker monitors or oversees the work done by the specialist worker.

The child protection worker is a case manager rather than a direct practice worker. In fact, in many countries the term 'case manager' is used to describe child protection workers. In other places the terms 'contracting out' or 'purchaser provider' rather than case management are used. Whatever terminology is used, however, the issues relating to the use of specialised services are present in child protection systems in most English-speaking countries.

What is the rationale for using specialist workers? The specialist workers can develop specific knowledge about particular problem areas or intervention methods—for example: drug use, mental illness, counselling, family therapy, family support, sexual abuse, violence, finances or parenting skills. With their specialist skills and knowledge they can work pretty much exclusively with clients who have problems in their specific area of specialisation. The concept is similar to going to a dentist for a toothache or a physiotherapist for a sore back.

As I discussed in chapter 1, however, the notion of the child protection worker as a manager rather than a direct practice worker has its critics. The criticisms have several common themes:

1. limited community resources and overburdened voluntary agencies can leave clients on long waiting lists, and sometimes without any direct service at all
2. the skills and morale of workers can be affected as their role becomes that of a manager with minimal direct or therapeutic client work

3. case planning decisions can be compromised when child protection workers are not fully informed about the client's situation because of a dependence on other workers for information

4. interventions by specialist voluntary agencies can lead to a symptom-focused approach to clients' problems, rather than a holistic approach

5. clients may be expected to repeat the same story over and over again to different specialist workers. (Hood 1997; Skehill et al. 1999)

As discussed previously, there is some research that supports these criticisms of case management. Hood (1997), for example, found in a United Kingdom study of local authorities that there were problems with mis-communication of information, duplication of roles, role confusion, and de-skilling and disempowering of workers. The statutory workers often felt de-skilled in terms of direct practice. Workers in the voluntary agencies, on the other hand, often felt disempowered in terms of decision making. I argued in chapter 1 and in my earlier book (Trotter 1999) that there are generic skills for work with involuntary clients, and clients need to be approached from a holistic perspective. The key to effective outcomes lies not in the workers' specialist knowledge but in his or her ability to engage the client and develop common goals.

To put it another way, there is an inevitable overlap in services if workers are using effective practices. An intervention by a drug counsellor, child protection worker, mental health social worker or family support worker will all involve a holistic assessment of the family situation and the development of goals and strategies to achieve them. The most successful interventions treat the person in his or her broad context—they do not focus particularly on one symptom or one problem.

Case management principles

Despite the problems associated with case management, contracting out and purchaser provider systems, child protection workers have little choice but to make the best of the system. What does the literature tell us about effective case management? Literature in this area is relatively sparse although a number of writers have referred to the importance of case management principles. Rubin (1985) in his review of effectiveness of social work practice comments that a common thread in studies dealing effectively with physically and mentally disabled clients was support for case management principles. Case managers followed up referrals, did case plans, made links with community resources and facilitated consistency in treatment. Anne Fortune (1992) considers the role of case management in the context of inadequate resources and points to the advantages for clients of a co-ordinated approach. She points to a number of studies which suggest casework outcomes are improved, for both voluntary and involuntary clients, when direct practice workers go beyond their 'comfortable' referral networks and when they have an understanding of bureaucratic procedures.

The clients' view of case management

Criticisms of case management receive some support in our study. It has already been shown in chapter 3 that the clients perceived case managers in the same group as investigators, supervisors and referral agents. They were also less positive about workers who they perceived as case managers compared to those who they perceived as helpers and supporters. The clients may, of course, have had their own perceptions of what a case manager is and this may have influenced their views. When they were uncertain it was explained to them that it involved referral, follow up and planning rather than direct service.

We asked the clients a range of questions about case management: How many agencies did they have contact with? To what extent did they follow through with referrals made by the workers? How did they fare in an environment of increasing demands for welfare services, often decreasing resources and the increasing tendency for workers to be case managers rather than case workers?

Most of the clients had been referred to other agencies during the period of their involvement with child protection. The likelihood of referral depended on the time the client had been involved with child protection. For example, of those who had been clients for more than six months, 85 per cent had been referred to at least one agency. On average, each client said he or she had been referred to three to four different agencies. Ten per cent had been referred to ten or more different agencies. The referrals were most commonly to family support agencies, foster care, general counselling, psychiatric assessment, sexual abuse counselling and drug and alcohol programs.

More than 80 per cent followed through with the referrals. In other words, the client had at least one contact with the agency. This percentage did not change markedly whether it was the first or the fifth referral, or whether it was a young person, a mother or another relative who was referred.

Clients gave a mixed reaction to the question about the extent to which referrals were helpful or unhelpful. The clients were asked to rate the referral on a scale of 1 to 7, with 7 being very helpful and 1 being very unhelpful. The average score on this question was 4.4, suggesting most clients found the referrals more helpful than unhelpful. The young people who were the subject of the child protection order were slightly less satisfied with the referrals (3.8).

In cases where the referrals were unsuccessful the clients gave a number of reasons—the most common being that their partner would not attend and therefore it did not work, that they did not need the referrals in the first place, or that they were unhappy with the worker to whom they were referred.

The workers' view of case management

I referred earlier to the idea that case managers should follow up referrals and work with referring agencies. We asked the workers to what extent they worked together with the referral agencies. They were asked to score 7 if they worked closely with the other agency and 1 if they had little or no contact with the other agency. The mean score on this question was 3.7 for the first referral and lower for subsequent referrals (3 on average), suggesting that generally workers did not work very closely with the other agencies. We also asked the workers to comment on how successful they felt the referrals were. They provided a mean score of 4.2. In other words, like the clients the workers felt they were successful a little more than half the time.

Client comments

Most of the comments made by the clients were critical of the referral process. In particular, many clients felt they were not consulted about the referral or they did not know what it was about.

I was not aware of the children being sent to the Children's Protection Society.

My worker referred me to lots of places but I don't remember what they were and I never went to them.

The children's mother wasn't going to ring rehab but the workers put the phone in her lap and forced her to ring a rehab agency.

The worker suggested occasional care and a financial counsellor, but she did not refer me to anyone.

I thought it was just for me to be assessed, but when I got to the Children's Court Clinic we were all there. I don't understand that—first just me, then the whole family. Then the children's court clinic said the children should be returned to their parents, but they did not identify the behavioural problems for the kids.

The worker arranged an assessment with a doctor. The doctor rang me and asked me what was going on as they were perfectly normal kids. I explained and he then said Billy may have an anger management problem but that was all. It was just a Mickey Mouse referral to satisfy the requirements of a court report.

The worker has given their mother the names of other people and places she can contact but the waiting periods are too long and their mother has given up.

The child is still not secure with the counsellor. It will take time to build trust. They are still in the process. We had to argue with the counsellor to make her keep seeing the child.

When we asked the clients to rate the helpfulness of the contact with other agencies they were reasonably positive. When they made comments about those contacts, however, those comments tended to be negative. The few positive comments the clients made were usually accompanied by negative comments. In the following example a mother was referred for assistance with housing. She obtained new housing but feels that nothing has changed.

Although we are not homeless in some ways it is worse now. Our new home does not address the problems of alcohol abuse by their father, in fact it hinders it.

Worker comments

The workers made few comments about the referral process, however, when they did comment it was about the problems encountered with referrals and other agencies rather than the positive aspects. They particularly commented on reluctant clients, workers from referral agencies who did not understand the problem, and the difficulty of making contact and securing appointments.

The father sabotaged the referral and simply refused to make contact after some time.

The mother and father felt the referral was successful, but the worker who they saw from the other agency disagreed with my risk assessment. This damaged my rapport with the family because they wanted to believe what the other worker was saying and not what I was saying.

To sum up, the clients and the workers expressed mixed feelings about the referral process. However, most of the specific comments they made about referrals were negative. It is interesting that the clients appear to have been little more satisfied with the services they got from the agencies they were referred to than they were with services from the child protection workers (the clients scored their satisfaction with the outcome of the child protection inter-vention at 4.3 and their estimate of the helpfulness of the referral at 4.4.). Given the tendency for the child protection workers to have a statutory and investigatory function and for the voluntary agency workers to have a helping and problem-solving function, this is perhaps surprising.

Interview observations

In the following interview a worker is discussing two referrals with a mother of three sons, two of whom have recently returned to live with her after a period living with relatives. In both cases the referrals were subsequently followed up by the family and the mother was very satisfied with the outcome of the referral. The mother was also reasonably satisfied with the outcome of the child protection intervention (rated 5 on the 7-point scale) and the worker felt that the family was progressing well (6 on the 7-point scale).

The mother Laura has a history of drug use and her family has been involved with child protection for about nine months. During this time the family has been referred to four different agencies. Here, the worker is in the process of making two of those referrals.

> Worker: What about this referral for family support? They can help you with parenting and things like that. It is voluntary.
> Laura: Is it like Julie who helped us before?
> Worker: Yeah, but we'll all sit down together and look at what sorts of things you want. She can say what she can help you with when you meet her. It is better you get it from her.
> Laura: I wonder how she can help?
> Worker: Maybe she can help you to be more assertive with the boys. She can be here at key times to see what you need help with—like in the mornings when they don't want to go to school—she can support you and give you ways to handle it. It's not easy and you've done well so far but they will keep testing and Nigel will probably be like the others as he gets older.
> Laura: I don't understand how she will help—when Max makes up his mind he's not going, he won't go.
> Worker: But she can give you some strategies. I know Julie helped you and Janet [from another agency] is still helping but she can't be here 24 hours a day. You've been trying, I know.
> Laura: It is a big adjustment to have two teenagers after being without them for so long—it takes time.
> Worker: I know. I spoke to Box Hill unit where you had the [drug] assessment. Any time you want to begin again you can contact them about the education for you and the children about not using [drugs].
> Laura: Yeah.
> Worker: I can't force you—that's voluntary.
> Laura: But the law has stated I have to do it.
> Worker: If you don't do it now you can do it later.
> Laura: I'd like to do it.
> Worker: Nigel has disclosed using marijuana and he needs help and

you need education about drug use. Their father may be using also and you don't want them exposed to that.

Laura: No.

Worker: I think they will be happy to go there and talk to the worker but you have to make the appointment so it will happen. Is there anything else you need help with—food, finances?

Laura: I have fixed up the bills and the food is fine at the moment.

Worker: The family support worker, probably Violet, will be able to help with the routines for housework and so on. It is hard when the kids are on holidays but the kids are old enough to understand that they can't just do what they want. We need to have a meeting so we can all discuss the situation—assuming the referral is accepted and Violet is the worker. We can talk about the issues of boundaries and limits and pocket money and so on. Do you want me to ring Doctor P. now [about the drug assessment]?

Laura: Yeah.

The worker picks up the phone and rings the doctor's surgery.

In this example the worker is involved in the referral process. She helps the mother understand its purpose and its voluntary/involuntary nature. She also plans to be involved in the initial meeting with at least one of the other agencies and is familiar with how both of the other agencies work. While I have pointed to the criticisms of the case management system, this example does suggest it can work well when the worker or case manager follows the sort of case management principles pointed to by Rothman (1991).

Case conferences

Another aspect of working with other agencies in child protection involves case conferences. It has been argued that outcomes for clients are likely to be better if clients and families and other professionals are prepared for and involved in case conferences, and if they are able to play a genuine role in the decision making (Farmer 1999; Holder and Corey 1986; Sinclair 1998).

Our study did not attempt to examine decision-making processes in any detail. It did, however, provide some interesting results in relation to case conferences from the viewpoint of the clients.

How do the case conferences operate? The case conferences are generally convened by a unit manager and usually include the child protection worker, a senior supervising child protection worker and other professionals involved with the family. The aim of a case conference is usually to make major decisions about the status of the client and to develop case plans.

Sixty-three per cent of the clients in our study indicated they had been involved in a case conference with child protection. We asked the clients a number of questions about their experiences of the case conferences. The clients were ambivalent about how helpful or supportive they found the conferences, most commonly rating the experience of the conference at 4 on the 7-point scale. For the most part they felt they were clear about the purpose of the conference although they were not very positive about the extent to which they were involved in the decisions made at the conference.

These views were, however, different depending on which family members were asked. The primary clients were least likely to have found the case conference helpful and supportive and least likely to have felt they were involved in the decision making, although they often felt other family members were involved in decision making. Mothers expressed similar views to the primary clients. Fathers and other relatives were the most positive about the case conferences.

It seems that those least directly affected by the decisions were most positive about the process of case conferences and those most affected, the primary clients and the mothers, were the least positive. On the other hand, regardless of how the clients felt about the case conferences it was clear that the more they saw them as supportive and helpful and the more they felt involved in the decisions the better the outcomes were.

When the clients described the conferences as supportive they were more than twice as likely to be satisfied with the outcome. The workers were also much more likely to believe the family was progressing well. Children were also significantly less likely to have been removed from the family home and the cases were significantly more likely to have been closed. Similarly, positive relationships with the outcome measures were evident when we asked the clients if they felt that they were involved in the decision making and if they understood beforehand what the conference was supposed to achieve. These differences were consistent and substantial and could not be explained by the risk levels of the clients.

It seems apparent that being clear about roles and working in a collaborative way leads to better outcomes whether working one-to-one with clients and client families or in decision-making forums, such as case conferences.

Client comments

Even though the clients rated the helpfulness of the case conferences at around 4 on the 7-point scale, most of the comments they made about the conferences were negative ones. Their concerns often related to not being aware of who was going to be at the meeting.

My husband was there and it ended up in a screaming match. If he hadn't been there it would have been fine.

When the whole family went it wasn't helpful. It is better if the worker speaks to family members individually because Dad argues if we say things and he doesn't agree. It was helpful when Dad didn't go. At the start it was intimidating as the worker would laugh at what I said. Later my attitude changed and I said what I wanted to no matter what.

I haven't been to the last few—I walked out. They were playing games—they didn't inform me who would be there [the paternal aunt was present] and the worker admitted they hadn't told me deliberately for fear I wouldn't come. They just sat and talked about the aunt having care of the child so I walked out.

Why do teachers and other people need to know our personal background. I wasn't aware that teachers would be there and that the workers had been to the school and talked to the teachers. It was intimidating having the teachers sitting there.

Some were concerned about follow up.

Case conferences appear to be helpful but nobody implements the decisions. Issues are spoken about but we never get minutes of meetings.

They had a whiteboard with my problems and goals. That was 12 months ago. At the time it was supportive but I followed the plan and they didn't return my child so it was not good. At the time it was '7' [on the scale] but it ended up unhelpful.

The few positive comments related to the opportunity to discuss issues.

Some of them were helpful—I was able to say things to my mother without fear of being thumped.

I felt like a stranger—I was really out of the discussion. Personally it was not helpful. They would be talking of things I didn't know about. But I did get to understand a bit of what was happening.

The supervisors seem very experienced and sympathetic. Each time we hoped they would let Jane come home. This did not happen but at least they could explain why the decisions were made.

Summary

Work with other agencies is an integral part of work in child protection. It is part of the process of dealing with client problems. However, there has been in recent times much criticism of the concept of case management. This criticism is based primarily on the idea that case management systems promote a focus on symptoms rather than promoting a holistic approach, and they lead to a fragmentation of the therapeutic relationships in which change can occur.

Our study provides some support for the criticisms of case management. The clients do not respond favourably to workers who they perceive as case managers, referrals are sometimes not followed up by clients and often not followed up by workers, and clients are little more satisfied with the services they receive from voluntary agency workers in comparison to services they receive from their child protection workers.

It is acknowledged, however, that this study does not provide any definitive conclusions about case management and that it does seem to work better when the child protection worker follows case management principles.

The clients were ambivalent about the helpfulness of case conferences. They seem to work best, however, when the clients were well prepared for them, when they knew who would be there and what to expect and when they were able to be genuine participants. There was a strong relationship between the client's view that the conference was helpful and supportive and all the outcome measures. It seems that well-handled case conferences are important to outcomes and this points again to the importance of partnership and collaboration between the workers and the clients in effective child protection practice.

6

PRO-SOCIAL
PERSPECTIVES

> The pro-social approach is about allowing a young person to have
> goals and expectations, to look at what they want to achieve and
> reward it, including the small steps. The worker should frame
> things positively. Let the client know if he or she makes mistakes
> and that some things are not okay, but still encourage him or her.
> Comment by a successful child protection worker.

I suggested in chapter 1 that the more successful child protection
workers are likely to use a pro-social approach. In my earlier
book (Trotter 1999) I described this approach in some detail and
discussed the theoretical and research support for it. The term
'pro-social model' is sometimes used to describe the four components of the intervention model outlined in this book: role
clarification, collaborative problem solving, pro-social modelling
and re-inforcement, and the client/worker relationship. This chapter
focuses on pro-social modelling and re-inforcement, a term I am
using interchangeably with pro-social approach. Below is a summary
of the four steps involved in this approach.

1. Identify pro-social comments and behaviours
Workers should attempt to identify pro-social or desirable comments
and behaviours during the course of interviews with family

members. While it is not possible to be prescriptive about what pro-social behaviours are, there are some examples with which there would be little disagreement. These include statements by parents that recognise the harm abuse of children can cause, statements that recognise children have feelings and developmental needs, statements that recognise the physical needs of children such as regularly changing babies' nappies, comments that suggest ways in which parenting skills could be improved or recognising there is a need for improved parenting skills, and comments that support a case plan developed in relation to the particular family.

Pro-social behaviours which could be identified are along similar lines; for example, parents changing nappies regularly, using non-physical means to discipline children, undertaking a parenting skills course, arranging access with an estranged parent, talking to a child about feelings, showing interest in a child's schooling or attending a case planning meeting.

2. Provide rewards
The next step in the pro-social approach is to provide rewards, re-inforcement or encouragement for the pro-social actions and comments. The most powerful reward or re-inforcer available to the social worker is praise. If, for example, a client attends a case planning meeting the social worker should make it clear that this is a good thing. Praise should be used liberally, however, it should be directed towards the pro-social comments and actions of the client. It should not simply be applied generally. The idea is to say to the client, 'It is good you were able to get here on time today and that you have been able to get to our last couple of appointments. It is clear you are taking the whole thing seriously', rather than simply saying, 'It is good to see you today'. The idea is to link the praise to pro-social behaviour and to reserve the praise for pro-social behaviour.

The child protection worker may use other rewards; for example, visit a family at home rather than the family visiting the office (or vice versa depending on how the family feels about this), spend time with family members or, alternatively, reduce the frequency of contact, visit at times the client specifies, provide financial assistance, or organise practical assistance, such as with home maintenance.

3. Model pro-social behaviours
The third aspect of the pro-social approach relates to modelling pro-social behaviours. Modelling pro-social behaviours involves the child protection worker modelling the behaviour that s/he wishes to foster in the client. For example, the social worker should be available when s/he is supposed to be or ring to change appointments, should treat the family with respect, should speak positively about her or his own children, and show empathy for the client's situation.

4. Challenge undesirable comments and behaviours
The fourth aspect of this model relates to the challenging of anti-social or undesirable comments. For example, 'I was only disciplining her', 'I only hit him because he kept crying', 'A good whack did not do me any harm when I was a child and shouldn't harm anyone today', 'I would change the nappies more often if I had a washing machine that worked'. The worker should also challenge anti-social behaviours, for example, inappropriate disciplinary actions by a parent.

The protective worker should then provide some level of negative re-inforcement. This might be as minimal as purposefully ignoring the behaviour or it might involve a very clear statement of disapproval. Care should be taken not to positively re-inforce anti-social comments through the inadvertent use of body language, as occurred in a study of the use of pro-social approaches in community corrections (Burns 1994). It was found that probation officers often inadvertently re-inforced anti-social and pro-criminal comments through the use of body language (e.g. smiling).

A number of studies have suggested that, while the more effective workers are likely to focus on the positive things their clients say and do, they are unlikely to minimise the nature of the abuse or neglect (Ammermann 1998; Gough 1993; Rooney 1992; Stanley and Goddard 1997; Swenson and Hanson 1998; Triseliot 1998; Trotter 1999). Nevertheless, it has also been suggested the corrections area, albeit rather arbitrarily, that workers should try to provide at least four positive re-inforcers for every negative one (Keissling 1982). An Australian qualitative study found that more successful probation officers focused almost exclusively on positives in contrast to less successful officers, who were more inclined to focus on negatives (Burns 1994). It seems important that disapproval and confrontation do not overwhelm the intervention.

The need for caution in relation to the use of confrontation is supported by Shulman (1991: 11), who states in relation to confrontation that:

> ... analysis of the data on the skills of confrontation thought to be crucial to effective social work practice did not yield the expected supporting results. When it occurs it seems to be important. Confrontation which comes too early in the relationship or which is not balanced by a large amount of positive comment may well have a negative impact.

Strengths based work

Pro-social modelling and re-inforcement is a strengths based approach. Dennis Saleebey (2001: 221) comments, 'The strengths perspective has many shades and hues—many different textures. It clearly is still developing ... not yet having the rigor of more mature theories, models, perspectives, or methods.' Nevertheless, strengths based work has certain common elements. It involves working with clients' strengths rather than their deficits. It is based on the belief that people learn more and progress better if their workers resist focusing on pathology and instead focus on the things their clients do well and on their achievements. It is based on the belief that even the most problem-saturated person has inner resources which can help him or her develop.

…001: 7) provides a practical illustration of …ased approaches in developing resilience in …people in care:

> … for practice is helping the person to hang on to …ositive factors, threads and niches in their lives. It ma… …bout tapping into the commitment of strong elements in the chil…s social network, for example a strong and interested grandparent who is willing to support the child in a different way.

Strengths based approaches are based on the notion that people will develop if there is a focus on the strengths in their lives, the factors which provide them with satisfaction, self-esteem and confidence. They are also based on the notion that people are more likely to learn and to make changes in their behaviour if they are rewarded and encouraged for the positive things they do and say rather than criticised for the negative things they do and say. The pro-social approach differs from some other strengths based approaches, such as solution-focused counselling, because it accepts that detailed problem exploration is an important part of the intervention process, and because it focuses on the pro-social actions and comments of clients rather than simply on strengths. The pro-social approach also accepts the need for some confrontation.

To give an example, using a strengths based approach a worker might focus on the development of self-esteem through attendance at a therapy group or involvement in a sport. The pro-social worker might, however, be more inclined to focus on child-rearing practices. To take another example, a young man might have a wide circle of friends who are very important to him. They might help to maintain his self-esteem and sense of identity. Using a strengths based approach the worker might focus on and encourage this supportive peer group. Using a pro-social perspective, however, the worker might take the view that because many of the young person's friends use illegal drugs and live on the streets the associations should not be encouraged.

I am not arguing that strengths based approaches do not focus on pro-social issues. The quote from Robbie Gilligan above clearly suggests they do. I am merely arguing that the pro-social approach highlights the importance of focusing on pro-social comments and actions in work with involuntary clients. It also provides a practical method of promoting pro-social values.

The pro-social approach, problem solving and risk assessment

I have argued that effective practice involves working with the client's view of the problem. What, however, if the risk assessment undertaken by the child protection worker points to one view of the problem and the client expresses a different view of the problem? How do you go about integrating the risk assessment and helping processes when the client, for example, is concerned primarily about finances and the worker is concerned about a mother's inability to carry out basic parenting tasks? The material presented in chapters 3 and 4 suggests that some workers do successfully integrate the two functions. The more successful workers certainly do not shy away from the investigatory or risk assessment role. On the contrary, they put energy into helping the client understand the dual role of the child protection worker.

The pro-social approach provides a method by which problem solving and risk assessment can be integrated. The risk assessment provides for the worker to systematically work through the client's history, the issues facing children and other family members, finances, employment and so on. It allows for a holistic assessment of the family situation. So the process of undertaking the risk assessment constitutes the beginning of the problem-solving process.

I suggested earlier that when the worker and client differ in relation to the definition of problems the worker should continue to work with the client's version until the client begins to accept the worker's view of the problems. This will often occur as the client and the worker explore the problem. For example, a father

might say he has a problem with accommodation but deny any problems relating to drug use. So the worker and the father begin to explore the accommodation issue. This may lead to discussions about previous accommodation or about finances. If drug use has proved to be a problem in relation to previous accommodation or finances this is likely to emerge in the discussions. The worker will then use the pro-social approach in rewarding any comments by the client that acknowledge the negative impact of the drug use. The worker may also confront the client in an appropriate way about the drug use.

The worker should be open with the client about the things which he or she wishes to encourage but continue to work with the client's problems. In some seminars I have undertaken workers have suggested working with two sets of goals or two case plans—one developed by the worker and one developed by the client. The worker's plan would distinguish between non-negotiable requirements, such as attending drug treatment or receiving regular visits from the district nurse, and the worker's goals for the client, such as reducing drug use, improving parenting skills or controlling anger. The client's goals or case plan would include those things which the client wishes to achieve, for example, new housing, a new relationship or help with finances.

The worker would then help the client to work towards his or her goals but at the same time use the pro-social approach to encourage the client to address the worker's goals. The worker would also make it clear that the non-negotiable things must be complied with and use the role clarification skills to help the client understand the process.

Use of the pro-social approach—positive re-inforcement

Generally speaking, the workers in our study tended to focus on client strengths or positives. We asked the clients if they were encouraged by their workers. On the 7-point scale they scored their workers at 4.3 on average. The clients also indicated they were not often discouraged by their workers, scoring this at 2.5.

When we asked how their workers encouraged them, almost half the clients commented that the worker praised their efforts, ideas or achievements. Forty-one per cent said their worker gave them praise when they acknowledged and took responsibility for a problem. One third also commented on the worker reassuring or showing confidence in them. Others pointed out that the worker visited them at home, or at a place which the client chose. Others commented on the practical assistance they received from their workers, for example, writing or telephoning someone on their behalf or making a referral to another agency.

Positive re-inforcement and client outcomes

When clients reported that their workers encouraged them the outcomes were good. For example, when the clients reported their workers had praised them for their efforts, ideas or achievements the clients were more likely to be satisfied with the outcome and the workers were more likely to be satisfied with the progress of the clients.

One very practical way in which a worker can encourage a client is by the variation in the level of contact. Again, when the clients indicated their workers had encouraged them or other family members by reducing levels of contact, the outcomes were also clearly better. Seventy-five per cent of the clients were satisfied with the outcome when contact had been reduced compared to 46 per cent when contact had not been reduced. The workers were also more likely to believe the family was progressing well.

On the other hand, when the client reported the worker had expressed doubts or reservations about the positive things they did, or said, or about their abilities and intentions, the outcomes were poor on each of the outcome measures.

Worker comments

Outlined below are comments about positive re-inforcement made by some of the more successful workers—those whose clients were satisfied with the outcomes of the intervention and who felt the families they supervised were progressing well.

It is about re-affirming family, providing support, not minimising negatives and emphasising possibilities, congratulating clients on attending meetings, or following up referrals.

It is just about re-inforcing positives, providing positive feedback and rewards.

It is about respect, courtesy, sensitivity.

I try to reward the client when any small gain is made.

The following comments were made by workers with poor outcomes—their clients were dissatisfied with the outcomes of the intervention and the workers were not positive about the progress of the families. While the workers often acknowledged the value of a pro-social approach, it is clear from the comments that they are not enthusiastic about it.

Often the relationship is set up to be a bad one by the nature of the work we do. You can do as much pro-social stuff as you like but if the parents won't come to the party it does nothing.

The pro-social approach is useful as long as you don't take it too far—for example, try to be too friendly, or focus on the parent rather than the child.

Time limits and family attitude affects how much you can do.

In court work, sometimes you can't be pro-social. My supervisor has said you can't be pro-social in a court report.

If there are lots of negatives I may focus on some but I let the others go to some degree, until later; otherwise it may seem we are giving them too much of a hard time.

My supervisor sometimes says, 'you can't be pro-social with this one, let Chris Trotter take it to court'.

To sum up, the comments by the more successful workers about positive re-inforcement emphasise the importance of focusing on positives, of respect and of courtesy but, at the same time, not minimising the impact of the abuse. The less successful workers, however, tended to focus on the difficulty of implementing the approach.

Client comments

Most comments made by clients about how they were encouraged were general ones. One mother who was positive about the outcome and made good progress according to the worker commented:

They have often re-affirmed that they don't have a problem with me as a parent.

Another mother, who was investigated following a report of abuse which was not substantiated, commented:

She apologised for how much she had upset me.

A number of clients felt rewarded by practical assistance:

She gave me a lift home from court when the children came back.

She tries hard to get assistance, for example, with finance.

She wrote a letter to the family court for us.

Others commented on how their worker listened to them:

> He encouraged me by listening to my problems, by being a friend.

> My worker encourages me by calming me down when I am pissed off. She listens to me.

> My supervisor was wonderful. When Jackie ran away from home Pam [the worker] just sat there with me. She would talk to us about our problems.

Even a perpetrator of sexual assault was able to comment on the positive attitude of the worker. This de facto father was very happy with the worker and the outcome, rating them at 6 and 7 respectively, although the worker was less positive about the general progress of the family, rating it at 4. The perpetrator continued to live with the family and the young person.

> She made me feel comfortable that this was an isolated incident. When allegations of molestation are made you feel like a molester. But she made me feel that this problem in our circumstances, with a broken family and so on, often happens and the department is not there to take sides or lay blame but to find out the truth. This made me feel more comfortable.

He went on to say:

> At first I thought they believed I was guilty—they were very stark and cold. So my initial reaction was 'they're lousy'. If I was an aggressive person I would have had my back up. But as the interview went on, the wall was broken. I would have preferred that her professionalism would mean she should not put me on edge as it did in the beginning. The other gentleman [secondary worker]—maybe years of the procedure had injured him—I don't think he cared one way or the other. He also repeatedly asked the same questions and did not listen to or remember my answers. The primary worker didn't forget anything and wrote it all down.

Negative re-inforcement and client outcomes

While the workers tended to encourage rather than discourage their clients, some clients indicated that their workers had been generally discouraging. Most commonly the clients felt their workers 'did not focus on their real problems', they 'failed to follow through with promised help', or they were discouraged by their worker asking them to 'do things they did not feel would be helpful'. Others were concerned about the worker not recognising their efforts or achievements, being criticised, or the worker making arrangements that the client felt he or she could not keep. Others were concerned about increased or excessive contact by the worker.

When clients felt their worker discouraged them and did not recognise their achievements or efforts the outcomes were particularly poor. Only 14 per cent were satisfied with the outcome compared to 55 per cent when clients felt they were not discouraged in this way. Similarly, the workers were less likely to report the client was progressing well, the cases were more likely to be open, and more than twice as many children or young people had been placed away from their families (24 per cent compared to 11 per cent).

The clients felt their workers discouraged them in this manner in only a small proportion of cases, however, this tended to happen with the higher-risk cases. The risk levels could not, however, explain the considerable differences in outcomes.

In each of the other instances, when the clients reported their worker had discouraged them we found poor outcomes. To use another example, when the clients felt their worker discouraged them by not focusing on their real problems they were less than half as likely to be satisfied with the outcome, the workers reported significantly poor progress, more cases were closed and more children removed from the home.

When clients indicated they felt discouraged by their workers those clients had particularly poor outcomes. In other words—the non pro-social workers did badly.

Client comments

Much of the anecdotal comments made by the clients about how they were discouraged involved not being listened to. A grandmother who was very dissatisfied with the worker and the outcome commented:

> Their timing was bad. The whole thing was pretty discouraging. They dropped the case when they needed to have it in hand, and took it up when she [the children's mother] was more sober. They did not believe me—particularly about my daughter's ex-husband being an alcoholic. The child protection workers were not trying to prevent harm to the child. Instead they were waiting for something bad to happen before they acted. I would understand and accept this if they said they couldn't get proof but it wasn't that—they just wouldn't believe me.

Others felt discouraged by what they perceived as a demeaning attitude from the workers. For example, a mother who was very unhappy with the worker and the outcome commented:

> I felt demeaned by their attitude and persona and the implication that we'd failed our child. Our whole family felt attacked and criticised that they were the cause of the problem when there was no real problem.

Other clients felt that they did not know what was going on, they could not understand the process or the role of the department had not been made clear to them. For example, a mother who was most unhappy with the worker and the outcome approached the department for help but felt that she ended up being investigated rather than helped:

> He was a nice guy, but I couldn't believe the position I was put in—I rang them for help and then I was investigated. They were checking up on my history from ages ago when I had some prob-

lems with the children and was reported to the department, but not checking up on my concern about who the child sees during access. Now I would try to fix things myself rather than going to child protection.

And another mother:

The story kept changing—I couldn't find out exactly what was supposed to have happened. It was not clear what child protection was going to do. They would say they were going to close the case then say they had to do more. The worker then did not send the closure letter because he said he had lost my new address.

One very dissatisfied mother even described her worker as abusive:

I experienced verbal abuse by the worker. She called me a junkie loser. She told the children I was a loser. She bribed my children to talk to her and then she dropped them.

It is clear both from the responses to the questions and from the clients' general comments that the more successful workers provided practical assistance, listened and acknowledged the positive things clients did. The clients with poor outcomes on the other hand felt their workers did not believe them, adopted a demeaning attitude and did not keep them informed about what was going on.

Pro-social modelling

According to the theory of pro-social modelling, if workers model appropriate behaviours their clients are likely to learn from those behaviours and they will in turn have better outcomes. In my earlier research in probation we found that pro-social modelling by the probation officer was influential in whether or not clients re-offended (Trotter 1996). It was also evident in the results reported in chapter 3 that when clients felt their workers completed tasks, a form of modelling, the outcomes were good.

Modelling pro-social behaviour involves, among other things, keeping appointments, being punctual and responding to phone calls. We asked the clients if their workers had kept appointments on time and if they responded to phone calls. Generally the clients felt their workers did keep appointments (average rating 5.5 on the 7-point scale) and did return phone calls (average rating 5.2). When the clients believed their workers had kept their appointments on time the outcomes were better. The clients were more satisfied with the outcomes, the workers felt the clients were progressing better and the cases were more likely to have been closed.

When the clients were annoyed by their worker's lateness, although this applied to only 40 clients, the outcomes were particularly poor. Those clients were about half as likely to rate the outcome positively and the cases were about half as likely to have been closed. Even the workers themselves were slightly less inclined to rate the progress of the clients positively when the clients were annoyed by the worker's lateness. The clients who expressed annoyance at a worker's lateness were higher-risk clients, however, this does not explain the significant differences in outcomes.

We found a similar trend when we asked the clients if their worker made phone calls when they were arranged and returned the client's calls. Again, we found strong associations with outcomes. The clients were almost twice as likely to be satisfied with the outcome, the workers were almost twice as likely to report the client family was progressing well, 40 per cent fewer cases remained open and 30 per cent fewer children had been removed from the home after 16 months. All of the associations are statistically significant. In other words, they were unlikely to have occurred by chance.

It could be that the more reliable workers had lower case loads or lower-risk clients and therefore had time to return phone calls and keep appointments. This could not, however, explain the differences. The case loads were reasonably evenly distributed among the workers and the risk levels were no different.

A few questions need to be asked here. Can it be that something as simple as keeping appointments and returning phone calls accounts for these substantial differences in client outcomes? Could it be that what might be described as simple courtesies are just as important, or even more important, than other direct-practice skills such as working through problems? It certainly seems so from this study. This study is not, however, an isolated one.

The importance of pro-social modelling is pointed to in a number of studies in corrections (e.g. Andrews et al. 1990). Two earlier studies of mine also provided similar outcomes, one with volunteer probation officers in juvenile justice (Trotter 1990) and another with professional probation officers in adult corrections (Trotter 1993). In both cases probation officers who scored high on a socialisation scale, a scale which measures the extent to which people are pro-social or pro-criminal in their attitudes, had clients with good outcomes. In both cases the clients were between 30 and 50 per cent less likely to re-offend if supervised by officers who scored high on the scale. One of the key characteristics of people with high scores on the socialisation scale is their reliability.

Client comments

The clients had little to say about this issue but the few comments they made confirmed the view that their worker's respect for their time was important to them:

> I was really upset when she missed our appointment because I had got myself really keyed up for it.

> The worker leaves everything 'til the last minute and then thinks the worse of you because you can't drop everything and be there. I have lost jobs because of the involvement with the department—from taking time off.

Confrontation

It seems clear that workers who model appropriate behaviours and who re-inforce their clients' pro-social actions and comments do better. Our study also provides support for what might be described as appropriate confrontation. We asked the clients: Was it clear what your worker wanted you or members of your family to do, what the worker was encouraging you to do and what the worker approved of? When the clients were clear about these things the clients were satisfied with the outcomes and the workers reported the family was progressing well.

We then asked the clients how their workers reacted if they (the clients) said or did negative things, for example, if they acted or spoke in an angry or negative way, or minimised the seriousness or impact of the problem on the child, or made excuses for their anti-social behaviour. The clients indicated the workers most often responded by exploring the reasons why they felt and acted that way. They also often pointed out the likely ill effects of such views or behaviour, or they suggested more positive ways of viewing the situation. They sometimes acknowledged the negative feelings were justified. Not responding at all or criticising the client were less common responses.

The response which related most positively to the outcome measures was that of suggesting more positive ways of dealing with the situation. When the clients suggested their workers responded in this way both the workers and the clients were more positive and the cases were more likely to have been closed. When the clients indicated their workers responded by acknowledging their negative feelings were justified the worker and client outcomes were also positive. The clients were again positive about the outcome when they felt their workers 'explored the reasons why they felt and acted in this way'.

When the clients reported their worker did not respond or react the outcomes were poor. More than twice as many clients reported they were dissatisfied with the outcome and the workers reported poorer progress among these client families. The outcomes were also poor when the clients said their workers pointed out the likely ill effects of the clients' views and behaviour or criticised the client.

It seems that the reservations expressed about the value of some types of confrontation may be well founded. The concern expressed about ignoring rationalisations and anti-social comments also seems well founded. The most successful form of confrontation seems to involve acknowledging the feelings of the client, suggesting more positive ways of dealing with the situation, and exploring why the client feels this way—rather than criticising or pointing out ill effects of the behaviour.

Client comments

Unfortunately the clients made few comments about confrontation and none about positive methods of confrontation. The comments they made were by dissatisfied clients and referred to inappropriate methods of confrontation. In the following example, an aunt who had been involved with the department for some years was unhappy about the worker and the outcomes. She felt dismissed by the worker:

> He insulted me. He was rude. He would not discuss things on the phone. He just cut me off. He looked down his nose at me as if I was a pathetic unreliable nuisance.

And another mother who was dissatisfied with the worker and the outcome said:

> She did not need to make me sit there and feel like I am a bad mother. How can I be a bad mother to one and good to the others. I felt my rights were taken away as a mother.

Observations

The interview transcripts shed some light on the effective ways of handling confrontation and the other aspects of the pro-social approach. In the following example a mother reported that she was very happy with the worker and with the outcome. The worker was also positive about the progress of the family. The family was assessed as of significant risk following incidents of domestic violence by the father, who is no longer living with the family. At the time of the interview the case had been open for more than six months. The mother Estha is bathing the children when the worker arrives.

> Worker: [commenting on work done on the house] Wow, isn't it great?
> Estha: Come in and have a look around.
> Worker: You've got blinds.
> Estha: I got them from the op shop. Look at the ones in the kitchen—they are not wide enough but it gets so hot in here. I'm worried it will get too hot for Depra.
> Worker: Were any of these blinds here before?
> Estha: No, I got them all myself.
> Worker: That's really great.

In another part of the interview the mother refers to her brother, who is now staying in the house. The worker is quite clear about what she expects, however; in the space of a few sentences she is able to acknowledge the mother's positives while making her expectations quite clear. She also offers positive ways of dealing with the situation.

> Worker: I understand he has a history of violence—charges for assault.
> Estha: So you know about that, do you?
> Worker: Yeah, it's our job to find out.
> Estha: I told you before he's been in trouble.

Worker: Thanks for being honest. But as the kids have been exposed to domestic violence we don't want it happening again.

Estha: He's mellowed a lot but I don't want trouble again.

Worker: We see it as a problem if he stays, but I understand you want to help him.

Estha: I feel a bit stressed—I have had to baby him, to drive him around.

Worker: You've been doing so well. There are also concerns about his possible psychiatric problems.

Estha: There is something wrong—he needs to be assessed. He did go somewhere, but I didn't get involved. I just spoke up for him in court because I did not want him to go to gaol. What should I do to get him to leave?

Worker: Tell him we are not happy that he's here. I'm also concerned this is ministry housing for you and the kids and if someone else stays it affects the rent. You could explain to him that you don't want to jeopardise the housing.

In another part of the interview the client begins to talk about her ex-husband, who had been very abusive towards her:

Estha: I'll never get involved with someone like that again. I can't believe I got myself into it. I've told him it is over. I don't want to put up with it.

Worker: Good on you. You've done brilliantly for yourself.

Estha: I know it's not my fault.

Worker: No, that is right, it was not your fault.

In the following example two children have been returned to their father after he spent some months in prison. He is unemployed at present and spends a lot of time gambling. He is very positive about the worker and the outcome, rating them both at 7 on the 7-point scale—although the worker rated the progress of the family at only 4. When followed up more than one year later the case had been closed. The worker and the father, Saul, are discussing employment possibilities. Ben, who is four years old, is in the room.

Saul: I'd like to do something more on leadlighting.
Worker: Are there any courses available that you know of?
Saul: There is one at the Chisholm Institute.
Worker: What about the neighbourhood community house?
Saul: Haven't tried it.
Worker: You could chase that up. You need to look at people doing renovations to see if they need help. Take a photo of this [a cupboard which Saul had leadlighted]. Maybe you could advertise in the local paper.
Saul: I was talking to a local fellow—he said to get photos.
Worker: Anything else you have made?
Saul: My sister has some lightshades which I did.
Worker: Fantastic. Get photos of them and put them together in an album and put something out there so you've got work to do. The department has no concerns about your ability to parent or your commitment to the children. The problem is about you. There's not a problem with your parenting. So it's time for you to take advantage of the stuff that's around.
Saul: I was talking to a bloke around the corner. He builds houses. He said, like you, to get photos. Lots of people say they can do things, but can't prove it, but I can do it and prove it with the photos.
Worker: You may be able to go to the demolition yards and glaziers to get broken pieces of glass you can re-use. I've done furniture restoration and I've learnt you have to keep at it. I can be working on a piece and then someone sees me doing it and they ask if I can do something for them. If people can come and see you working on something they see you can do it. There's a number of things you can do and ways you can get into it.
Saul: Come on, have a piece of toast [offered to child who refused].
Worker: He may not want solids. He was getting into the Weet-Bix® before.

Saul: I've been looking for other jobs—in Frankston—at a shoe factory—I have done that before.

Worker: At the moment, to get you into the mainstream you do have to pull out all stops.

Saul: I shouldn't be sitting on my arse.

Worker: I don't think you are sitting doing nothing, but it's hard.

Saul: It is hard.

Worker: The thing is you can't help getting bored—that's about space in your life, about not having space filled.

Saul: Yeah, it's true. I've got all these great ideas rattling in my head. Should I go out and do it or wait for the child to get older?

Worker: Both. Do some now, do what you can but accept that you won't be able to do more than you can do. But the stuff you do now you can do and may do more later.

[Father went out to check on Ben, who was very quiet.]

Worker: You have the advantage of knowing the days the child is in creche.

Saul: You think I'm doing a good job?

Worker: You know I think you're doing well.

Saul: I just need to hear it.

Worker: It's not the parenting—you make that look easy—you do it so well.

Saul: Really?

[Ben is getting restless.]

Worker: Yes. Do you think I should go now?

Saul: Yes, he's getting restless.

Worker: What I'd like to do is see you next Wednesday when I've had time to chase things up for you.

The repeated re-inforcement of the father's good parenting skills is a feature of this interview. The implied message seems to be 'you are doing well with your child and I would like to help you with other issues in your life'. In this and the previous interview the worker is quite lavish in her praise for the client, for example, 'That is really great', 'That is fantastic', 'You have done brilliantly for yourself". The comments appear to be accepted as sincere by the client.

The interviews we observed provide few examples of inappropriate ways of talking to clients. As mentioned earlier, the more effective workers tended to volunteer to have their interviews observed. However, in the following example the clients, Sacha who is 14 years old, and her mother were only moderately happy with the worker and the outcome. The client rated the satisfaction with the outcome at 4 and the mother rated it at 5. The worker also rated the progress of the family at 4.

The participants in this interview were referred to in chapter 4. The worker is trying to focus on why things are going well now compared to previous occasions, however, the focus tends to be on the negative factors rather than reinforcing the positive things that the clients have achieved.

The worker enters the house with Sacha after collecting her from school. Sacha's mother Tina is preparing carrots for dinner.

Worker: Both of you said things are better so this is a good opportunity to explore why.

Tina: She's doing alright.

Worker: She sure is. I'm keen to work out why things are better and plan for the possibility of things going down again in future.

Tina: She's more settled. She was running to Allan all the time.

Worker: What do you reckon. Why are things better now?

Sacha: I don't know.

Worker: If you don't know why it is better, do you know why it was wrong before.

Sacha: No.

Worker: I am sure you've got some ideas. What do you think [to mother]?

Tina: I think it's an anger problem.

Worker: Your mum said some really good things about your home-

> work. It seems, however, that when you get stressed you need someone
> to support you with school.
> Tina: Yes, she seems to need help.
> Sacha: I don't know about a lot of the schoolwork. The others know.
> Worker: How do they know?
> Tina: They [the teachers] can't get through to her. But I might ring and
> talk to the teacher. I'll ring tomorrow.
> Worker: That would be great.

Summary

The research suggests that child protection workers are likely to be more effective if they re-inforce the positive and pro-social things their clients do, if they model appropriate behaviours, and if they make appropriate use of confrontation.

When clients indicated their workers made use of these skills those clients tended to do better on each of the outcome measures used in the study. When the clients believed their workers were in the habit of keeping appointments and returning phone calls the outcomes were a lot better. Confrontation was most effective when the worker suggested more positive ways of viewing the issue or explored the reasons why the clients felt and acted in that way. It was least effective when the worker did not respond, pointed out the likely ill effects of such views and behaviour or criticised the client.

It seems that simple modelling processes, such as returning phone calls and keeping appointments, are very important factors in client outcomes, even to the extent of whether children are removed and cases discharged. The impact of such basic worker skills is rarely discussed in the counselling or child protection literature, however, there is some other research support for their importance. This has major implications for the day-to-day practice of child protection workers.

7

RELATIONSHIP BUILDING SKILLS

> More than anything—be honest. Be punctual. Don't collude. Be
> clear all the time and bring them back to the issues you are dealing
> with. Be a real person, have some fun with them, don't wear a
> heavy tin hat, don't have a heavy-handed approach. Be hopeful.
>
> Comment by a successful child protection worker.

Child protection practitioners and policy makers often make
the comment that the key to effective practice lies in the
'relationship'. By this they mean that somewhere in the interaction between the worker and the client lies the potential for
change. The academic literature, however, defines the relationship more narrowly (e.g. Compton and Galaway 1999).

The 'relationship' has been defined many times over many
years. Helen Harris Perlman (1957), for example, talked about
the client/worker relationship more than 40 years ago in her book
on social casework. Since that time a multitude of helping texts
have examined the relationship (e.g. Compton and Galaway 1999;
Hepworth et al. 2002). Most of the texts suggest that the
worker/client relationship has certain elements. These usually
include the worker's empathy, or ability to understand what the
client is saying and feeling. Empathy is manifested in reflective
listening, which refers to the workers' reflections, paraphrases and
summaries of client comments. Other elements of the relation-

ship include issues of authenticity, confidentiality and openness, self-disclosure and the use of humour. The notion of expectation and client motivation is also often addressed as part of the client/worker relationship. Sometimes confrontation is discussed under relationship, although in this book I have discussed confrontation in chapter 6 as part of the pro-social approach.

Empathy

Much has been made of the importance of empathy in counselling relationships. Lawrence Shulman (1991), in his child protection study, cited a number of relationship factors which were related to positive outcomes. He found that workers who 'reached inside of silences, put client feelings into words, displayed understanding of client feelings and shared worker feelings' did better (Shulman 1991: 44). Their clients viewed them as more helpful, their clients spent less days in care (away from their parents) and they were less likely to go to court.

On the other hand, the results of some studies of empathy with other types of involuntary clients have been more mixed. A study undertaken by Don Andrews and his colleagues (1979) found that probation officers who scored high on a psychological test of empathy had clients who offended more often than expected. Similarly, probation officers who made use of reflective listening practices in taped interviews had clients who offended more often. When those officers also made use of problem-solving and pro-social skills, however, the probationers offended less often than expected. It may be that empathic responses in the absence of pro-social modelling and re-inforcement can be interpreted by clients as acceptance of their anti-social behaviour.

My own work on the effectiveness of empathy in probation found that volunteer and professional probation officers who had high levels of empathy did no better or worse than probation officers who had low levels of empathy. This was the case in studies using psychological tests of empathy (Trotter 1990; 1993) and measurements of the use of empathic comments in file notes (Trotter 1993; 1996)—although the one finding that was significant in this study related to the use of judgmental comments. When workers made judgmental comments in files notes (e.g. 'lazy', 'no hoper') clients offended more, even after risk levels were taken into account.

Some work has been done on the use of empathy with other groups of involuntary clients. Andre Ivanoff and his colleagues (1994) cite several studies undertaken with a range of involuntary clients that point to the potential of a genuine, empathic, helping relationship to be overwhelming and even aversive. William Nugent and Helene Halvorson (1995) also found in role-played interviews that 'inappropriately worded paraphrasing' of client comments could 'elicit anger, anxiety and depression in clients'. The authors favour an approach involving the provision of possible alternative interpretations of the client's expressions rather than simply reflecting what the client has said.

Empathy and the outcome measures

Our study nevertheless provides some support for empathy. We asked the clients, 'Has your worker understood your point of view and the way you feel?' When clients responded positively to this question they were more satisfied with the outcome (67 per cent compared to 32 per cent when they responded negatively to the question), the workers reported more positively on their clients' progress (60 per cent compared to 40 per cent), and the cases were more likely to have been closed (65 per cent compared to 56 per cent).

We also asked the clients to comment on the 'things you appreciate about your current worker'. The item commented on most often by clients was that the worker 'listened to my views and problems'. Sixty-one per cent of the clients commented on this factor—more often than other factors, such as the worker was 'courteous and respectful' (54 per cent), or the worker 'recognised that I was doing my best' (50 per cent), or the worker 'kept appointments, returned phone calls and rang when planned' (50 per cent).

The clients were also asked what were the things 'you did not appreciate about your worker?' The issue identified most frequently was that the worker 'did not understand our family's real problems'. This was commented on by 24 per cent of clients—more often than the worker being 'too busy and not available when needed' (23 per cent), or the worker 'focused too much on one problem at the expense of others' (20 per cent), or the worker 'cancelled appointments and did not return calls when planned' (19 per cent), or the worker 'made us do what the department wanted and was not relevant to the family viewpoint' (19 per cent).

The outcomes were also poor when the clients identified their workers as not listening, not understanding the family's real problems or focusing too much on one problem at the expense of others. To take one example, when the clients identified that their worker 'did not understand our real problems', those clients were satisfied with the outcome in only 23 per cent of cases in comparison to 60 per cent where they did not identify this issue. The workers reported the family was progressing well in only 35 per cent of the cases compared to 56 per cent and more children were removed (17 per cent compared to 11 per cent).

The results are even more compelling when the clients identified the worker as critical and judgmental, perhaps the opposite of not understanding the clients' real problems. When workers were seen by their clients as critical and judgmental those clients did much worse on each of the outcome measures.

While the research is equivocal about the value of empathy, this study certainly suggests that understanding the client's point of view is important. It may be, however, that the empathy which is effective is not the explicit use of reflective listening skills but more subtle ways of understanding and listening to the client's story. As discussed later, our study lends some support to this interpretation.

Worker comments

The following comments were made by workers who felt their clients were progressing well and the clients were satisfied with the outcomes.

I try to be non-judgmental, to define the problems together with the client, to show respect to clients.

I like to treat them as you would want to be treated yourself—develop a relationship, get to know their story, work therapeutically with them, be consistent, be on time, allow enough time for visits.

It is about effective listening, engaging without colluding, a relationship with balance rather than power.

Good practice is about unconditional positive regard, but with no colluding or minimising.

I believe in respect, listening, being honest, following through, giving positive feedback, keeping them informed and regular contact. I take a client-centred approach, which is respectful of what they want. I spend time with them, getting to know them, giving some of myself, some self-disclosure, so it's less threatening and not all one-sided. I talk about my parenting. I acknowledge rituals/birthdays, Christmas cards.

And some comments are by workers who did not do so well with their clients:

The courts often force us into seeming to blame.

I focus on letting them know what my expectations are.

Client comments

While many clients were positive about the intervention when asked to complete the rating scales, when they made comments in the interviews they tended to focus on what workers did wrong.

The comments below provide a few examples of clients who felt they were not listened to or understood. In each case the clients were unhappy with the outcomes and the worker felt that the progress was poor.

When people come to the department for help, they should have a special department for those [voluntary] people. The way they treated me I could easily have suicided except for the kids. To get help, I had to tell them things that they could write down and then they used them and they looked bad in a report. In an earlier involvement, I was concerned about my husband's violence but the department still allowed my violent partner to stay. They had incorrect information. They went to court and said that I was on methadone and coping well when in fact I was not on methadone and I was not coping. I asked them for help and they walked away. I recognised I needed help and they acknowledged that I recognised it, but they didn't give me the help. I have never been referred to a domestic violence group.

In the following case the client was happy with the worker and with the outcome, but unhappy with the way things happened. The worker was also happy with the progress of the family. The client's comments, however, focus on the way things happened.

They're a large government-funded organisation to help families. I wish they could be more helpful in a 'real' way. Every family they see must be different, but the workers need to be more flexible and find out the problems completely before just attacking the parent—'We need to do this investigation on you' because someone complained. I wouldn't mind if they came and they cared about the problems we faced. I don't like them just landing on the doorstep. The first initial impact should be as non-threatening to the parent as possible. They should ring the parent first. They need to consider that there may be a context to what has happened. The mother may be swearing at the kids because of some situational problem. Their disapproval is threatening, I feel like telling them to piss off and I get angry with them. They need to change their image—that they are there to be helpful. Their reputation is shit. People seem to have negative views about them—I don't know anyone who likes you [to the researcher]. They are investigative; they are not helpful or supportive. First impressions are lasting impressions and the first visit is crucial. You feel like you are a criminal—when what you need is a cuddle, not a notification. The workers need to be more useful to families. It should be about 'family protection', not child protection. I didn't get proper parenting. My mother ran away. I try to do the best I can. If I make mistakes I need help, not to be dragged into court.

Observations

The interviews which we observed revealed little of the reflective listening techniques referred to in the textbooks (e.g. Carkhuff 1969; Hepworth et al. 2002). As I mentioned earlier, the interviews tended to be conversational and mostly involved exploring problems. In fact, in more than 60 pages of transcript from the 13 interviews we observed the research officer was able to locate only five instances of reflective listening. The transcripts do indicate that the workers for the most part understood the clients' point of view, however, the workers rarely made use of the reflective listening techniques of paraphrasing and summarising. When it did occur it was often accompanied by the worker expressing his or her own view as in the following example.

Worker: Ben has serious problems. I know how much you love both boys and are committed to doing your best for both of them. I think it's difficult for you at times to keep control and take control. I hear you saying you want Josh to go away and Ben to be home, but I am not sure it's best.

The following example is one of the few in which a stereotypical reflective comment is used by the worker:

Mother: He is much happier now he has his bike. When I pick up the girls, Mike comes to the car to say he's heading home and we drive and he rides.
Worker: Sounds like you have a good routine.

Self-disclosure

There is some discussion about self-disclosure in the helping literature. Dean Hepworth and his colleagues (2002) suggest, for example, that while there is little agreement about the amount of self-disclosure that workers should offer, some research suggests the detached, cold and distanced therapist may be particularly unhelpful. They go on to argue that an authentic or real approach by workers is likely to be most helpful.

While self-disclosure has received less attention in the child protection literature, Lawrence Shulman (1991) did consider the issue in his Canadian child protection study. I referred earlier to the example Shulman used of a young worker asked by a middle-aged mother if she is married and has children. Shulman suggested an appropriate answer in this circumstance would be, 'I'm not married and I don't have children. Why do you ask? Are you concerned about my being able to understand what it is like for you raising three kids?' (Shulman 1991: 45). He suggests that this type of response is more likely to be associated with positive outcomes than a defensive or secretive response.

The clients' view

Does our study shed any light on the issue of worker self-disclosure? The clients did not seem to see self-disclosure as very important. When we asked the clients what they appreciated about their current worker only nine per cent indicated they appreciated the fact the worker 'used his or her life experience to help me'. We also asked the clients what they did not like about their workers and only 14 per cent responded that they did not like the fact their worker was impersonal and would not reveal anything about him or herself.

While the issue of worker self-disclosure does not appear to be one which is of major concern to clients, when the clients did comment on a worker's self-disclosure, the outcomes were better on each of the outcome measures. The clients were almost twice as likely to report the outcome as positive; for example, when they indicated that some self-disclosure had occurred. Similarly, when the clients indicated they did not appreciate the impersonal approach of the worker the outcomes were poor.

The workers' view

We asked the workers what type of self-disclosure they believe is usually appropriate in their child protection work. Fifty-seven per cent of the workers saw it as appropriate to talk about their interests and hobbies; for example, I am a keen tennis player or gardener. Slightly less (51 per cent) felt it was appropriate to comment on their own personal life experience in exploring problems and strategies; for example, a comment like, 'I have found that admitting mistakes often helps me in my own relationships'. Fewer (43 per cent) felt it was appropriate to talk about their own situation in terms of whether they were married or had children, and fewer again (40 per cent) felt it was appropriate to comment on the demands of protective work or their feelings about the work; for example, 'I don't like having to come in here to tell you someone has made a report about you'.

The workers' views about self-disclosure related significantly to only one of the outcome measures. When workers indicated they favoured each of the examples of self-disclosure their clients were less likely to have been removed from their families and placed in the care of the department. For example, when workers indicated they were opposed to self-disclosure in terms of revealing their marital status or information about their children, children were removed from the families on 19 per cent of occasions. When they favoured self-disclosure the children were removed in only 5 per cent of cases.

Given that it relates to only one of the outcome measures and that there is no other research to support such a startling finding, it is certainly premature to suggest the lack of worker self-disclosure is a factor in whether children are removed. It could be simply that when workers are required to place children away from the family they become more impersonal.

Observations of the interviews

Neither the workers nor the clients had much to say about self-disclosure and there were few instances of worker self-disclosure in the client/worker interviews. Some of those instances are outlined below. In each case the clients were positive about the worker and the outcome and the workers were positive about the progress of the client's family.

In the following, taken from one of the interviews referred to in chapter 6, the client, Saul, has been talking about seeking work in furniture restoration.

> Worker: You may be able to go to the demolition yards and glaziers to get broken pieces of glass you can re-use. I've done furniture restoration and I've learnt you have to keep at it. I can be working on a piece and then someone sees me doing it and they ask if I can do something for them. If people can come and see you working on something they see you can do it. There are a number of things you can do and ways you can get into it.

This is an example of a worker talking to a mother:

> Worker: Have you found out your rights as a tenant? I have a little booklet as I'm renting myself.

Another worker commented to a mother:

> Mother: The time is going—it will be 2010 before we can blink.
> Worker: Don't say that. I'm supposed to have a baby by year 2000.
> Mother: You need a man first.

And another conversation with a mother:

> Mother: See the scratches on his legs—they are mosquito bites—you have sensitive skin too.
> Worker: Yes, I don't even know I'm scratching—it's a skin condition.

This worker is talking to a young person who is starting a course. In this instance the young person is not so happy with the worker or the outcome, rating them at 3 and 4 respectively.

> Client: They won't help you. At the start they asked if I have a disability, but it's not like school—you have five minutes to do it and I can't do it.
> Worker: No, it's not like school. What took me a long time to work out and I did just before I finished my degree—is that they treat you like an adult and you have to ask for help.

It has been argued previously that self-disclosure which relates to workers' difficulties rather than to their achievements is likely to work better (Masters et al. 1987). This might explain why the reference to the worker's university study was associated with poor outcomes. It maybe that self-disclosure, which relates to the worker's achievements, can make the client feel inadequate and in turn lead to poor outcomes.

Openness and honesty

Much of the literature on the client/worker relationship suggests the worker should be open and honest. The workers should be open about issues such as how their authority might be used, how information about the clients might be used and who might have access to it.

Generally, the clients felt their workers were open and honest. In fact 70 per cent of the clients indicated they found their worker open and honest. Also, when we asked the clients what things they appreciated about their current worker, 49 per cent identified the worker's openness and honesty.

Honest and open workers did better with their clients. When the workers were identified by the clients as honest and open, 70 per cent of the clients were satisfied with the outcome compared to 35 per cent when the client did not identify the worker as honest and open. The worker's estimates of client progress were also better.

The importance of being open and honest was further supported when we asked the workers to rate themselves on the extent they were open and honest in their dealings with clients. When they believed they were open and honest the outcomes were better.

Unfortunately, the workers and the clients had little to say about this topic. The comment referred to at the start of the chapter seems to sum up the type of approach which leads to good outcomes:

> More than anything, be honest. Be punctual. Don't collude. Be clear all the time and bring them back to the issues you are dealing with. Be a real person, have some fun . . . Be hopeful.

Motivation

> You can't help someone to change if they don't want to.

> A person must accept that they have a problem before they can address it.

> People change when they are ready to change and not before.

Comments such as these are common among welfare professionals. Certainly the worker with a large case load of difficult families might take some comfort in the notion that he or she cannot be expected to work miracles with an unmotivated family. This concept also has some support in the literature. Jones and Alcabes (1993), for example, argue that readiness to change is fundamental to positive outcomes in child protection and other involuntary clients.

On the other hand, it is often argued that client motivation is heavily dependent upon the interaction between the worker and the client (e.g. Compton and Galaway 1999; Hepworth et al. 2002; Moyers and Rollnick 2002). It may be that client motivation is, as much as anything else, a factor of the relationship between the worker and the client.

The concept of motivation is difficult to define—it has many levels. For example, at the lowest level, a father who is prone to angry outbursts with his children may simply deny these outbursts occur. On the other hand, he may accept they occur but argue they do not harm the children and are therefore not a problem. Or he may accept they occur and accept they may harm the children, but argue that he cannot control his feelings and that the children provoke him. Or he may say he wishes to change his behaviour but then fail to take any action in this direction. Or, finally, at the highest level of motivation, he may accept he has a problem and genuinely attempt to address it.

Assessing levels of motivation is difficult to do, partly because clients will often be motivated at different levels at different times. They may be in denial one minute and motivated the next. In our study we used a few different measures of motivation. We asked the workers to rate the extent to which they believed their clients were motivated to address the issues which had led them to become involved with child protection and the extent to which the client was willing or ready to change. We asked the worker to rate this both at the time the client was initially allocated and at the time of the interview with the research officer.

There was a very clear association between the workers' estimates of the client's motivation and the outcomes. When the workers felt their clients were motivated to change they felt that those clients progressed better. Similarly, the clients were more satisfied with the outcome. This was the case whether the workers commented on the current motivation of the client or reflected on their motivation at the time the case was allocated.

The clients, however, had a slightly different view. We asked the clients, 'At the time when child protection first visited, to what extent did you or others in your family feel that things needed to change (i.e. in relation to the problems identified by the worker or the subject of the notification)?' We anticipated that those who believed things should change, the more motivated clients, would have more positive outcomes. This, however, was not the case. There was no clear relationship between the clients' views that they were motivated to change and the clients' satisfaction with the outcome, the worker estimates of the progress of the family, case closure or removal of children.

When the worker judged the clients to be motivated those clients did better. Not only did they do better in the view of the workers, they also did better in the view of the clients. However, when the clients felt that things needed to change it made no difference to the outcomes. What does this mean? Perhaps workers are better at assessing client motivation than the clients themselves. Or maybe the client's view, that he or she needed to change, does not necessarily reflect a willingness to work towards change.

Expectation

The notion of motivation is related to the notion of expectation. Motivation is about the wish to change. Expectation is about whether change is anticipated or expected. While there was no relationship between the clients' expressed level of motivation and the outcome measures in this study, there was a strong correlation between the clients' view, that they expected the worker would help, and the outcome measures. When the clients expected the worker to help they were twice as likely to be satisfied with the outcome and the worker was also more positive about the progress of the family.

We also asked the clients the question a bit differently: 'Does your worker believe you and/or your family will be able to make positive changes so that the problems will be reduced?' When the clients responded positively to this question they did better on both the worker and client outcome measures and their cases were closed earlier.

It seems, therefore, that the clients do well when their workers feel they are motivated to change. The clients also do well when they believe their workers can help and when the clients feel the worker believes in their potential to change. It seems the more effective client/worker relationships are characterised by a mutual belief in each other. The comment 'You can't change someone who does not wish to change' might be better expressed as, 'You can't expect someone to change if you don't believe in his or her potential or if he or she does not believe you can help'.

The results of our study in relation to motivation and expectation are generally consistent with the findings in the rest of the study. Outcomes are generally better when workers have a helping orientation and when they talk about their helping role. It is perhaps not surprising, therefore, that clients do better when they expect their worker will help and when their worker sees them as motivated.

I mentioned in chapter 1 that the results I am reporting in these chapters cannot be explained by the risk levels of the clients. So while the more motivated clients and those who the workers expected to do well were lower risk, this is not sufficient to explain the findings of the study.

Worker comments

The following comments were made by workers who did well with their clients. In other words, they (the workers) felt their clients were progressing well and the clients were also satisfied with the outcome of the intervention. It can be seen that the workers are optimistic about their clients' potential to change, however, this optimism is tempered by a degree of reality.

> I have some families where I personally have no optimism, but make an attempt to appear optimistic to the client and offer services in the hope of change.

> I believe that everyone has it in them to change; although I am wary of being too optimistic—you may lose sight of other things, and that can be a danger. I say optimistic things to clients; but I also acknowledge barriers.

And one worker who did poorly with her clients said:

> I've become cynical after time in the job. How optimistic you can be depends on their past history also.

Client comments

The following comments were made by clients who were satisfied with the worker and the outcomes. One young person said:

> My worker treated me like a human being. The previous worker had a 'children should be seen and not heard' attitude, and gave me lectures for making mistakes.

A mother commented:

> I expected that they should have been there to help. Both of my workers said they were there to help. But in reality, the second worker was more professional and confident and was able to see the 'big picture'. The first worker couldn't see the big picture.

Interview observations

The following two excerpts from interviews illustrate how optimism and expectation are manifested in practice. The first example includes additional excerpts from the interview presented in chapter 6.

The mother's children are on a supervision order following reports of domestic violence. Her husband has now left home. The client, Estha, indicated she expected that the worker would help and she is optimistic about her chances of making positive changes.

Estha: I'll never get involved with someone like that again. I can't believe I got myself into it. I've told him not to wait for me. I don't want to put up with it.

Worker: Good on you. You've done brilliantly for yourself.

Estha: I know it's not my fault.

Worker: No. You want to see Janene [her daughter, who is in care]?

Estha: Yes, but it's holidays. I want to do group work.

Worker: Have you got the phone numbers? I can give them to you.

Estha: I can get the number for the domestic violence outreach. If you speak to someone who's been through it they understand.

Worker: That's good—not that the worker has been through it, but that she understands. The question remains—how to arrange access [with the children's father]. We could use the police but it does not make for a nice environment.

Estha: I want to have a normal life.

Worker: You want to move on. You may need to use a public place to drop them off for access, maybe McDonald's®.

Estha: Is that okay?

Worker: Yeah, it's better in public.

Estha: I said he could come to my parents—is that okay?

Worker: As long as they are there.

Estha: I wish he would support the kids more.

> Worker: I know you do. Nevertheless, things are going well and we're very pleased.
> Estha: Except I am worried about Dean [her husband].
> Worker: Yes, I know. However, we want to help the family. If you continue to be protective toward the children it will be okay.

In this interview the worker re-inforces the client's strengths: 'you have done brilliantly'. She also acknowledges the client's wish to move on and she is optimistic about the children: 'it will be okay'.

In the following example the client provided lower ratings to the questions about whether she expected the worker to help and about whether the worker believed she (the client) could change. In each case the rating was 4 on the 7-point scale. Clearly the interviews have a different purpose and the relationships between the workers and the clients are different. Nevertheless this interview is clearly less encouraging and optimistic.

> The worker has called into the home of a grandmother who is caring for her daughter's two children.
>
> Worker: I'm really just here today to see how you are and how Brony is.
> Grandmother: I'll get her up—she's been asleep.
> [Grandmother went to get the child.]
> Worker: How are you, Brony?
> Grandmother: This is a new look she has [hair in curls]. I don't think she'll go to you.
> Worker: Can we try? Where's Nanna—is that what she calls you? Where has Nanna gone?
> Grandmother: She's getting to be a big girl.
> Worker: She is. I can't believe it.
> Grandmother: She eats like a horse. Whatever you are eating she likes what you are having.

Worker: So she eats anything.

Grandmother: Anything! Which means she'll even eat what's on the floor.

Worker: What's happened with the pediatric assessment?

Grandmother: You have to write that letter.

Worker: Oh! What I thought . . . we'll see if we can get a new letter.

Grandmother: I can go tomorrow.

Worker: Is it the same doctor who you saw the last time?

Grandmother: No. I'm weaning away from him—you have to wait an hour. If you go to the clinic it takes three minutes.

Worker: What did the doctor say?

Grandmother: About her chest? She went over her with a fine tooth comb and said she's clear.

Worker: Is she still crawling and standing on chairs?

Grandmother: She was walking before she went back to her mother and then her mother put her in the walker and she stopped.

Worker: I've seen her walk at her mother's. Has the doctor seen her walk?

Grandmother: No.

Worker: That's something a paediatrician could check. But you think she's okay?

Grandmother: Oh, yes.

Worker: So she's walking, sleeping, eating, and you think she's okay?

This interview is different to the earlier interview in that it does not contain any optimistic comments or any positive re-inforcement. The first sentence of the interview sets the scene with the worker saying 'I am just here to see how you are', rather than talking about how she might help.

Humour

There is some reason to believe that humour can be a constructive factor in child protection work and that the appropriate use of humour can contribute to the development of the client/worker relationship, and in turn to more positive outcomes. There has been some discussion about this in the social work and therapeutic literature. Max Siporin (1984), for example, in an article called 'Have you heard the one about social work humour', argues on the basis of several research studies that humour can ' . . . provide an emotionally arousing dynamic for confronting, provocative insight giving and empathic helping procedures' (Siporin 1984: 461). He goes on to suggest that humour can be used to help clients deal with and distance themselves from problems and diffuse anger.

David Pollio (1995: 378) argues in favour of the therapeutic benefits of humour in crisis intervention settings. He suggests that 'positive outcomes of humour include breaking an impasse in the therapeutic process, reframing the context of the problem situation, freeing and empowering the client system and humanising the situation'.

Lawrence Shulman (1991) found in his child protection study in Canada that child protection workers who had a sense of humour (rated by their supervisors) were more likely to be viewed by their clients as helpful, skilful and trustworthy. Their clients also had fewer admissions to care and fewer court appearances.

The value of humour is supported by the results of our study. We asked the clients, 'Does your worker have a sense of humour?' When the clients believed that their workers had a sense of humour they were more positive about the intervention. Sixty-eight per cent of the clients were satisfied with the outcome when they believed their worker had a sense of humour compared to 32 per cent when the client did not think the worker had a sense of humour. When the clients felt their worker had a sense of humour the workers were also more positive about the progress of the family (61 per cent compared to 39 per cent).

Worker comments

The workers did not have much to say about the use of humour. In seminars I have undertaken with child protection workers I have also found the workers reluctant to talk about humour—perhaps because the humour that occurs in child protection interviews is often subtle and it emerges spontaneously. It is about lightness, smiles and sometimes laughter, rather than about jokes, funny lines and uproarious incidents.

One worker who did well with her clients—in other words she felt that generally her clients were progressing well and her clients were generally satisfied with the outcomes—commented:

> I use humour where it is appropriate—it is to do with good natured-ness.

Another worker, whose clients had poor outcomes, commented:

> I won't joke with them but I am happy to have a laugh together.

Client comments

The clients also made few comments about humour. The following comments were made by clients who had good outcomes. The first by a young person:

> 'She's a dickhead' [in a friendly way].

A comment by a mother who was dissatisfied with the worker and the outcome saw the worker as humourless:

> I made a bet with the family that I could get the worker to smile; and I did!

Observations

The following comments are taken from the observations of the interviews. In each case the client and the worker were positive about the intervention and some humour is apparent in the interview. In each case the humour is part of a light and friendly interaction.

Worker: Have you found out your rights as a tenant? I have a little booklet as I'm renting myself.

Mother: Yeah, there is so much information around; but it's a landlord's market. But I saw a good one the other week—furnished, three bedrooms, spa in the bathroom—and it was only $180 per week.

Worker: You wonder if it could be rat infested [laughter].

Worker: Oh, I knocked this over [a toy which was on the table] and don't know how to put it together.

Mother: Oh come on, you've done all that study.

Worker: Where did it come from?

Mother: It came out of a Kinder Surprise® [chocolate] packet.

Worker: Well, there you go—I don't eat enough Kinder Surprises®.

Worker: Have you seen much of Michael and Allen?

Mother: Yes, they were here on Wednesday night. It was Michael's birthday.

Worker: How did you celebrate?

Mother: We had snaggers and sausage rolls—here, at home.

Worker: What are snaggers?

Mother: Sausages [laughing].

Worker: So I learned something new today!

Jane: I am saving at the moment.

Worker: What are you saving for?

Jane: To buy some Crayola® pencils.

Grandmother: About $60 worth.

Jane: Maybe by my birthday I will be able to afford it. Maybe if someone gives me $10 [with a look at her grandmother and general laughter].

Worker: Are they the scented pencils—do they smell?

Jane: Yeah—licorice, orange, lemon, lime, and I think there's strawberry. I want to get them before school starts.

The exception to the rule

Perhaps the major criticism of evidence-based research is that it purports to provide one answer. As I discussed in chapter 1, it is sometimes argued that evidence-based approaches downplay diversity and treat people as if they are all the same.

In our study we observed 13 interviews between clients and their workers. We had hoped to do more and those that we did tended to be with the longer-term clients and with the workers who were well regarded by their clients and positive about their work. In each instance when the outcomes were positive it was clear in the interviews that the worker was using at least some of the relationship skills and the other effective practice skills that have been the subject of this study. There was, however, one notable exception. In this interview the worker displayed some relationship skills but few, if any, of the other effective practice skills which have been discussed in this book. Yet on the outcome measures the client did well (although the worker did not do so well with her other clients, who on average rated their satisfaction with the outcome below the study average).

The following interview appears to be confrontative, directive, sometimes negative and judgmental, and it offers solutions to problems without any apparent problem exploration or goal setting. Yet the worker indicated she was happy with the progress of the family and the mother indicated she was very happy with the worker and the outcome, rating them at 6 and 7 respectively.

This family has been supervised by the worker for more than six months. The family was initially assessed as significant risk and the worker has been visiting fortnightly. The interview begins after the worker has introduced the research officer and the mother, Svetlana, has introduced her daughter, Lina to the research officer. The worker, the research officer and the mother then go into another room.

Worker: This room gets too cold. You need some rubber-backed curtains—we've talked about that.

Svetlana: I've been looking.

Worker: No you haven't, but that's okay.

Svetlana: If Alex [who shares the house] moves out I will move into his room—although that breaks the lease because the lease is in Alex's name.

Worker: Why? You go to the estate agent and re-negotiate it.

Svetlana: They've told me they won't.

Worker: Obviously they don't want to go through the rigmarole. Explain to them your friend is buying a house but you want to stay on here.

Svetlana: I've told them.

Worker: What did they say?

Svetlana: They said they're not prepared to break the lease—I told them I have a friend wanting to move in and we would have no trouble with the rent.

Worker: What did they say?

Svetlana: They're not wanting to break the lease.

Worker: What're you going to do?

Svetlana: I am just waiting.

Worker: Don't. Go to the tenant's advice bureau. The estate agent is only telling you what they want. Have I only come here to listen to what you haven't done—feel free to arc up here [laughing].

Svetlana: No, I've done a lot.

Worker: Sounds to me like you need to have a round table—I'm willing to be there—with everyone saying what there is to gain or lose.

Svetlana: I've tried to get sense out of Alex but it is not happening.

Worker: Before you moved in we discussed you living on your own. It was your choice to go in here. If this doesn't work you may need to revisit the discussion.

Svetlana: I have already discussed getting a two-bedroom flat with Alex.

Worker: So not going in as partners—just sharing?

Svetlana: Yes. Everything in this house is mine except the washing machine.

Worker: Can we move away from the washing machine [the washing machine is making a noise]?

[They moved to a quieter room as the worker interacted with the child.]

Worker: She's looking well. Look at those gnashers [teeth]. Hello little sweetie. She's looking so much older—more childlike and less toddler-like. Okay. So, let's go through some of the checklist—literacy?

Svetlana: I haven't spoken to Rosemary—she's on holiday.

Worker: So are you joined at the hip and you can't do anything for yourself?

Svetlana: No, I have been so busy with what's happening in the house.

Worker: Am I embarrassing you—I hope I am—I get tired of this. Simon is not always around to read for you.

Svetlana: I have made an appointment with the counsellor.

Worker: You mean the psychiatrist?

Svetlana: Yes, the one you gave me. And I went to the doctor about two to three weeks ago.

Worker: What did you get from the doctor?

Svetlana: I can't pronounce the name—I will get the packet—Zoloft® and Stelaze®.

Worker: How are you finding this?

Svetlana: Fine.

Worker: Why did you have to get more? Were things too much for you?

Svetlana: I ran out. And things were getting pretty bad.

Worker: I don't know how many times I can say this but you need to take the literacy stuff seriously. You won't be able to do it in a few short workshops. There are issues ahead around the family court and we [the department] may not be involved. I'm not second-guessing your relationship with Simon. It seems very good and sound, but you can't rely on Simon. You must be able to read and write for yourself, otherwise you will have to rely on people and that makes you vulnerable—both you and your child. You don't want to expose Lina to that sort of risk. I don't understand what the blockage is.

Svetlana: Since moving here things have been on edge.

Worker: They always have been. Can you see a time in future when they won't be on edge? You have a bright active child and you will have to keep on your toes. If you think you'll have a free time in future it won't happen—you just have to fit these things in. I'll be out of your life. If you can't prioritise it, you're stuffed. You'll have to rely on the Alexs and Simons of the world to negotiate everything for you. It's an enormous issue. Potentially more damaging to your child than anything else. You've done such a great job and provided such a great environment for her. If you say it's too hard one of three things will happen. She'll hold herself back for you; you'll have to rely on others; or you'll have to muddle along. If a teacher sends a note home, you'll have to wait for someone to come to read it and rely on their interpretation. It's a big threat; you can't do anything without doing it.

Svetlana: Yeah.

Worker: I'm not just talking about reading bills—there's lots of other more important documentation you need to be able to read. On another subject—the young mother's program playgroup. It is a bit loose and informal but it has the skills based stuff—you can go when you want. I rang a whole lot of places—and I strongly advise you to go to it.

This interview is directive and the worker is lecturing rather than collaborating. However, it does include some humour, the worker does appear to have a genuine concern for the client and there are a number of instances of positive re-inforcement. In fact, the worker makes it clear she feels the client is doing a 'great job' with her daughter. The worker is also involved in tasks. She has rung up about the young mother's program playgroup and is happy to be involved in the round table. The worker has also been involved with this family for more than six months and it seems that a degree of warmth has developed between the worker and the client.

Nevertheless, it is not the type of interview one would expect to lead to good outcomes. I have included it because reporting the results of the study would have been somewhat biased without it. It also serves to illustrate there are times when workers with excellent skills have poor outcomes and times when workers with poor skills have good outcomes. It also suggests good practice skills are sometimes subtle ones and not necessarily consistent with prescriptive approaches.

This study has focused on the general principles of good practice as they apply across a range of situations. This interview points to the idea that the fit between the style of the worker and the style of the client might also be a factor in outcomes. For example, a directive and confrontative style might lead to good outcomes for some clients in some situations, particularly if it occurs within a well-developed and trusting client/worker relationship. Hopefully more light will be shed on this issue in the future as more studies examine the relationship between worker/client interactions and client outcomes.

Summary

In our study the workers generally demonstrated good relationship skills. When workers made use of the various relationship skills the clients generally did better on the outcome measures. The clients saw the worker's ability to listen and understand their problems as particularly valuable. These qualities were also related to improved outcomes. When workers were judgmental and critical the outcomes were particularly poor, with more than twice as many children being removed when the workers were critical.

Self-disclosure, humour and openness are qualities valued by the clients and generally related to improved outcomes. These qualities or skills were not much in evidence, however, in the interviews we observed. The observations also revealed few instances of reflective listening, paraphrasing or summarising.

It may be that the interviewing skills expounded in text books and taught in universities are utilised infrequently in day-to-day practice. Certainly it seems that many workers were able to give their clients a sense they were being listened to without using these techniques. This could be because in most cases they were long-term clients or it may be that their more conversational styles are more genuine and more appropriate. This study cannot resolve this issue but it certainly points to the need for more examination of worker/client interviews in order to develop knowledge about what works and what doesn't. There seems little point in teaching these skills to students and practitioners if in practice they are infrequently used and other more conversational styles achieve the same purpose. This issue is discussed further in the next chapter.

The concepts of motivation, expectation and worker optimism seem to be important ones in child protection. They each relate to client outcomes. The results of this study challenge the view that you can't change someone who does not wish to change. It seems that child protection clients are most likely to change when the worker thinks the client can change and the client thinks the worker can help. This suggests that the likelihood of change may be as much a factor of the worker/client interaction as the apparent initial motivation of the client.

STAFF SUPERVISION AND WHAT THE EVIDENCE TELLS US ABOUT GOOD PRACTICE

It seems clear that workers who make use of certain skills do better with their clients. It might also be anticipated that those workers who have good skills and good client outcomes would enjoy their work more. It might also be anticipated that staff supervisors who model and encourage effective practice skills would foster those skills in their staff. Staff supervisors with good skills might even have good outcomes among clients within their teams.

These issues are addressed in this chapter. I then go on to discuss what the study tells us about what child protection workers actually do, the differences in the responses between different types of clients, the extent to which the findings apply to other countries and settings, and the limitations of the study. Finally the discussion returns to the case study referred to in chapter 1 outlining some guidelines which might help Margaret, the child protection worker, to deal with Mr Pope and his two-year-old daughter, Sophie.

Worker satisfaction

On the whole the workers in this study were reasonably happy with their work and gained satisfaction from it, rating it at 4.8 on the 7-point scale. They were happier, however, when they indicated they made use of the effective practice skills.

When the workers said they make use of the skills of role clarification, collaborative problem solving, pro-social modelling and re-inforcement and the worker/client relationship they indicated they were particularly 'happy with their work and get satisfaction from it'. When they gave high ratings on their use of specific skills, such as establishing whether abuse had occurred, establishing whether clients understood what they were there for, understanding the clients' definition of the problem, using humour, discussing rationalisations and rewarding positives, they were also happier and more satisfied with their work. When workers believed their clients have the capacity to change they were again happier and more satisfied with their work.

Not only is the use of effective practice skills good for clients, it is also good for workers. What about the supervisors?

The supervisors

The focus of this study has been on worker skills and how these relate to outcomes. Staff supervision is another factor in the equation. The study did not consider staff supervision in any detail, however, we did ask the workers a number of questions about the extent to which their supervisors modelled and encouraged effective practice skills.

I anticipated that if supervisors model the practice skills of role clarification, collaborative problem solving and the pro-social approach, this modelling would influence the practice skills of their workers, the workers' satisfaction with their supervision, and in turn the outcomes for clients. There is some evidence from other studies that good supervision can lead to better outcomes for clients. Harkness and Hensley (1991), for example, found in a small study that when supervisors regularly asked their staff certain questions, such as what is your client hoping to achieve or what does the client understand is the purpose of your work, their clients were satisfied with the staff interventions.

It is often argued that first-line supervisors in child protection reflect the forensic and investigatory focus of many child protection services. Judith Gibbs (2001) found in her study, for example, that supervisors often focused on accountability and policy issues rather than reflecting on their workers' skills and experiences. They also often focused on the workers' failures rather than their successes. She also found that staff turnover and worker satisfaction were related to workers' experiences of supervision.

In our study, however, the workers were generally positive about their supervision. They generally felt their supervisors were non-blaming, open and honest, understanding of their thoughts and feelings, optimistic, and able to use humour in their work. They also suggested that their workers offered at least some discussion about their role as supervisors. The workers felt their supervisors generally modelled appropriate behaviours and rewarded their workers' good work and ideas. They also tended to be non-confrontative—although the workers felt their supervisors were not inclined to use problem-solving processes with them.

Not only did the supervisors tend to use effective practice skills with their workers, the more they used the effective practice skills the more the workers were happy and satisfied with their work. When workers, for example, indicated their supervisors had discussed their role as a supervisor, their expectations and their authority, those workers were more likely to be happy with their work and to get satisfaction from it. Similarly, when workers felt their supervisors identified the positives in their work, rewarded and encouraged them for good work, and modelled positive attitudes and behaviour, they were happier and more satisfied than in cases where their supervisors did not do these things.

The workers were also happier if their supervisors addressed problems with them, if they were open and honest, understood their thoughts and feelings, were optimistic and were able to use humour. The workers were, however, like the clients, somewhat equivocal about confrontation by their supervisors. Workers were no more or less happy and satisfied when they felt their supervisor was prone to confront them over negative actions or comments.

Not only were the workers happier if their supervisors modelled good practice but the workers were also more likely to make use of the skills of effective practice. When the workers reported their supervisors made use of role clarification skills they reported they were inclined to focus with their clients on establishing whether 'my client understands what we are here for'. Similarly, when the worker reported their supervisor used the skills of pro-social modelling and re-inforcement the workers were inclined to focus on rewarding positives and strengths in their clients. When the supervisor addressed problems, the workers focused on understanding the clients' problems and when the supervisor displayed relationship skills the workers focused on being human, using occasional humour and on understanding the clients' definition of the problem.

Hence, when workers indicated their supervisors modelled the effective practice skills they were happier and more satisfied with their work and more inclined to use the skills with their clients. We might, therefore, expect a link between supervisors who modelled the skills and good outcomes for clients within their teams. In other words, good supervision might move down the line to good client outcomes. This tended to be the case. When supervisors modelled the skills the workers generally reported their clients were progressing well. This was not at statistically significant levels, however, and it did not relate to the other outcome measures. Perhaps there are too many intervening variables to find a clear relationship between supervision and client outcomes. The workers' and the supervisors' levels of training, education and experience, for example, might all impact on the associations between the variables.

The supervision of staff involves more, of course, than simply modelling good practice skills. Supervision has an important

educational role for example. The focus of our study has, however, been on the skills of the worker and how they relate to the outcomes for clients. How those skills can be taught through supervision and training is a subject for another day, although there is some evidence that the skills of effective practice can be learnt (Trotter 1993). Nevertheless it seems fair to say at this stage that supervisors who model effective practice skills are more likely to have workers who use those practice skills.

While the workers were generally positive about supervision when asked to rate their experiences, the few additional comments they made tended to be negative. The following comment by a rather dissatisfied worker with relatively poor outcomes summarises some of the difficulties of working under poor supervision.

> We should focus more on the best interests of the child—sometimes children disappear into the system, the bureaucracy. There is a lack of resources, competing needs of other family members, lack of time by workers to investigate, lack of money, and so on. Supervisors sometimes undermine workers' assessments of clients. They will tell the worker 'this is high risk', and direct workers to respond in ways other than the workers' own assessment would indicate. Some supervisors are very controlling—you can see the case is high risk and your supervisor tells you to close, or you see it as low risk and the supervisor, who was not there with the family, tells you it's high risk. The experience is also different with different cases and with the supervisor's mood. And then the unit manager may get involved and case loads and other pressures become a factor. Workers are often not allowed to express their feelings about their cases or their jobs, as it would immediately affect the supervisor's view of their performance. This then affects their own perceptions about the job. From my observation this happens to others in the team. Sometimes if you try to be open about these concerns to your supervisor, it can cause problems and affect how they feel about you and your loyalty. Yet if you don't talk about it you become unsatisfied.

What the study tells us about what child protection workers do

We have seen in the earlier chapters that the clients on the whole felt their workers made use of at least some of the effective practice skills. For example, a majority of clients felt their workers had discussed the purpose of the intervention and their (the clients') real problems. A majority felt their workers encouraged them and were clear about expectations. The workers also felt on the whole that they made use of the skills. However, when we examined the transcripts of actual interviews between the workers and the clients we found the interviews seemed to be very conversational and contained a lot of what might be described as problem exploration.

Some of the child protection workers told us anecdotally that they made a habit of displaying the steps in the problem-solving process on their office walls. They indicated they would sometimes give clients copies of the steps as they explained the process to them. We did not, however, see this in any of the 13 interviews we observed.

The interviews contained some examples of worker empathy, of positive re-inforcement and encouragement, and of humour. There were few examples, however, of discussions about the dual role of the worker as both a helper and investigator, few discussions about setting goals and strategies to achieve them, and few examples of confrontation. Often it was hard to distinguish where the interview was heading or how it fitted with an ongoing intervention plan. Yet, as I have mentioned, these were no doubt the best examples of child protection interviews. The workers who participated in the interviews had undertaken specific training in the practice skills addressed in this study and they would no doubt have been keen to display those skills in interviews observed by a research officer. We might expect to have seen greater use of the skills in these interviews than we might have seen in a random selection of interviews.

These were longer-term contacts for the most part and this might explain the lack of structure in the interviews. In 1969, Reid and Shyne found in a study of child welfare that short-term contacts provided more structure—in other words, more goal setting, problem definition and so on—and for that reason they were more effective (Reid and Shyne 1969). It may be that had we observed interviews in the short-term team we would have seen more of the skills we were looking for.

If the skills had been applied more faithfully the outcomes might have been better. There is some evidence that program integrity is an important element of effectiveness in work with offenders (Andrews 2001). In other words, programs or interventions applied in a way that is consistent with a particular model or theoretical orientation work better. This is an area ripe for further research—the difficulty of accessing interviews notwithstanding.

It is difficult to draw any firm conclusion from a sample of 13 interviews. Nevertheless, it may be that the use of these skills is a more subtle process than some social work and helping texts might suggest (e.g. Hepworth et al. 2002). Empathy, for example, might be more about body language and silences than about paraphrasing and summarising. The text book teachings on reflective listening might be more academic exercises than practical guides for practice. While it is clear that defining problems, setting goals and developing strategies leads to better outcomes, the manner in which this occurs in order to achieve those outcomes is less clear. The actual practice of problem solving might be subtle and conversational.

What the study tells us about the different responses from different client groups

For the most part the different client groups in this study expressed similar views about the skills of the workers and the outcomes.

However, there were some differences between the primary clients and the mothers, the fathers and the other relatives or friends.

The primary clients had a different view to their parents about being removed from their family and placed in foster care, for example. The young people were positive about the outcome of the intervention when they were placed away, whereas the parents were negative. Other relatives were more equivocal. Relatives and young people were generally more positive about the outcomes than mothers and fathers, particularly fathers. Young people and the relatives were more inclined to see the workers as helpers, counsellors and problem solvers and less likely to see them as investigators. The primary clients and other relatives were also more positive about the workers' skills. Nevertheless, regardless of which client group was examined, the relationships between the use of the skills and the outcomes were apparent.

I referred in chapter 1 to the importance of cultural issues in child protection. The workers felt that in about 11 per cent of cases the client's cultural background or his or her limited knowledge of English was a factor in the child protection intervention. In these cases the relationship between the skills and the outcomes continue to be evident. The relationships are also evident in instances when clients are intellectually or psychiatrically disabled. They are also evident whether the client is a young person, a mother, a father, another relative or a carer, and whether the concerns are about physical, sexual or emotional abuse. It does not seem to matter who the client is, they all appreciate a worker who is clear about his or her role, understands their problems, is clear about expectations and focuses on positives.

Are the results of the study applicable to other populations?

Child protection in the eastern region of Victoria in Australia is different to child protection in the rest of the state. Child protection in Victoria is different to the rest of Australia, which in turn is different to other parts of the world. So it is important to ask whether the results of this study apply to other places.

The short answer to this question is that we learn from information from a wide variety of sources. Every group of people is different. If this sample had been taken one year earlier or in another region of Victoria it might have given different results. In developing the evidence base for practice we rely, however, on information from different times and from different places. We can never consistently know definitively what works for a particular person at a particular time. However, we have more faith in knowledge which is derived from populations similar to our own.

It is interesting to consider, therefore, what type of child protection service is offered in the eastern region. Is it one of the more forensic services that Parton and Byrne (2000) talk about, or is it more a helping or therapeutic service?

Some indicators suggest the eastern region is more forensic in its approach. Children and families in the Victorian system may not be seen on a voluntary basis. In other words, if child protection wish to stay involved with a family after a period of investigation they must take the family to court and have a court order imposed. Child protection workers are referred to as case managers and much of the therapeutic work is carried out by voluntary agencies. Only child protection services may take children to court, not voluntary agencies. Risk-assessment training is offered to all child protection workers and workers are expected to complete a risk assessment on all families with whom they become involved.

On the other hand, prior to the study commencing most of the child protection workers had undertaken a one- or two-day training course in effective child-protection practice, a course that focused on the helping rather than the investigatory aspects of the work. There is acknowledgment at all levels of the organisation that the client/worker relationship is important in child protection work. The majority of child protection workers in the eastern region are social workers or welfare officers and have been educated in assessment, counselling and social justice issues.

The child protection service in this study is clearly more forensic than many of the European services, which place minimal emphasis on proving abuse, use the courts only as a last resort and focus predominantly on welfare issues (Heatherington et al. 1997). On the other hand, it clearly has a welfare or helping orientation in addition to its forensic aspects. It is perhaps middle of the road in English-speaking countries in terms of its forensic/welfare orientation.

Limitations of the study and areas for further research

In chapter 1 I talked about a number of the limitations of this study: It could be considered narrow in that it does not take into account the myriad of other factors which might impact on client outcomes; only a little over 50 per cent of the clients we wished to interview were in fact interviewed; the outcome measures were limited and in some cases subjective; only 13 interviews were observed. I attempted to counter each of the arguments in chapter 2, nevertheless, as discussed before, it is clear that one study in one place, no matter how sound the methodology, cannot demonstrate that one approach necessarily works better than another in all or even most circumstances.

However, the skills which appear to work for workers and clients in this study are the very skills that have been seen to work in many other studies. As I pointed out in chapter 1, the skills identified in this study are the skills the research suggests are the most effective. They are also the skills I have found in two previous research studies (Trotter 1990, 1996) to be effective in the supervision of involuntary clients.

This study has not found out anything new by showing that certain worker skills and approaches are related to good outcomes, although in chapter 1 I pointed to some commentators who doubt it. It has confirmed, however, what many have argued: these skills do work and that good skills can lead to improvements in client outcomes by as much as 50 per cent (Andrews et al. 1990; Reid 1997; Trotter 1999). It has also, I hope, helped the reader to develop some knowledge about the specific nature of the particular skills.

Critical incidents and the media gaze

In chapter 1 I referred to the pressure placed on child protection services and child protection workers when individual cases have been highlighted by the media. I referred to several children in English-speaking countries who had died despite the fact they were receiving services from child protection workers and a range of other professionals. These critical incidents have helped to bring child protection services into disrepute and in some cases ruined the careers of individual child protection workers.

Newspaper reports seem to suggest that a forensic approach might be the best method of reducing the frequency of these incidents. The theme seems to be—if only a proper risk assessment had been done and the child removed the tragedy would never have occurred. The evidence from this study seems clear, however, that effective workers do not have a forensic focus. They have a balanced approach, which involves doing the investigative things including risk assessments and removing children when it is necessary. It also involves, however, a focus on helping the client to understand the role of the worker and simultaneously attempting to understand the client's point of view and work through a problem-solving process.

Our study does not provide specific information about the effectiveness of workers in reducing the frequency of critical incidents. One child died in the 247 families in our study and there were six cases of attempted suicide. Each critical incident is a tragedy in itself, however, from a statistical viewpoint the numbers do not allow for any conclusions to be reached.

Several factors do suggest, however, that the use of the evidence-based approach advocated in this book will lead to fewer critical incidents than a more forensic approach. The results from the study clearly indicate that use of the model is related to the workers' view that the family is progressing well in relation to the presenting problem—in other words the original form of abuse. It is also related to the clients' views about the outcome. In some cases it is related to earlier case closure and fewer children being placed away from their families. In other words, the balanced investigatory/helping approach which this study advocates appears to be effective in reducing child abuse. It seems fair to assume that it is also likely to be related to fewer critical incidents; that is, fewer incidents of very serious child abuse.

There is one other important reason why the model is likely to lead to a reduction in critical incidents. One of the best ways to protect children from the risk of critical incidents is for the worker to be in possession of the maximum amount of information about the child and the parents or carers. This information is more likely to be available if the clients feel they can trust the worker. Trust is developed through a partnership rather than an exclusively forensic model.

I referred earlier to a case example which involved a child's death which may have been prevented had the voluntary agency worker had the power to enter a client's home. I also referred to several child deaths which may have been prevented if the roles and responsibilities of different workers had been clearer. I have argued for a holistic approach to child protection work, for minimising the number of workers involved and for a co-ordinated approach to work with other agencies. This study suggests that around 20 per cent of the child protection referrals were not followed up at all by clients. The clients felt the referrals were generally no more helpful than the interventions offered by the child protection workers. And the workers tended not to follow them up to see if they were providing a useful service. It seems likely, therefore, that the more holistic and co-ordinated approach advocated in this book might reduce the number of critical incidents.

Guidelines for child protection workers

In chapter 1 I discussed the dilemmas faced by Margaret, a child protection worker who was working with Mr Pope. Mr Pope had physically abused his two-year-old daughter, Sophie, and Margaret was unsure how much she should be confronting Mr Pope about what he had done. She was also unsure about whether working in partnership meant working with his unacceptable value system and how she could reconcile her risk-assessment role with her helping role.

The focus of this book has been on how to help people like Mr Pope to change (which will in turn help Sophie). What guidance can the findings of this study give to Margaret in this process?

- Whether she is working with parents, children or relatives, she should try to balance her investigatory and helping roles. She should be very careful not to adopt an exclusively forensic role, even with severe high-risk families.

- In using a balanced approach she should talk about her role as both as an investigator/helper and talk about the purpose of the intervention. In particular she should talk to Mr Pope about how she will go about helping him with his problems and encourage him to accept her as someone who can help.

- She should be very clear about her expectations, about what is negotiable and what is not negotiable. She should carefully monitor Sophie's situation to ensure there is no repetition of the abusive behaviour.

- She should encourage Mr Pope to define the specific and real problems or issues he faces. And she should try not to underestimate the seriousness of those problems. She should, however, encourage him to focus on risk-related issues—in other words, the problems which led him to become a client of child protection.

- She should encourage Mr Pope to set specific goals. She should work with him to develop ways or tasks to achieve the goals and she should complete some of those tasks herself.
- She should try to maintain ongoing contact with Mr Pope and, if she needs to, refer him to other agencies. This should be done as part of the problem-solving process. She should also maintain contact with the other agencies.
- She should prepare her clients for case conferences and support them in those conferences.
- She should be lavish with her praise for her client's pro-social achievements and comments. She should be clear that when she is giving rewards, such as reduced contact, that this is because of her client's progress.
- She should take great care to keep appointments and to respond promptly to phone calls. This alone might make the difference between a positive and negative outcome.
- While she should be clear about her expectations she should be very cautious about confrontation. When she does use confrontation she should focus on positive ways of dealing with the situation. She should be very careful about being critical and judgmental.
- She should try to be open and honest about the child protection process and not be afraid of some self-disclosure.
- She should take an optimistic view of Mr Pope's capacity to change and acknowledge that his motivation will be influenced by her own skills and expectations.
- She should not be afraid to use humour, but it will be a subtle form of humour and lightness.
- She should use these skills in a way which comes naturally to her.
- She should find a supervisor who models the skills of effective practice.

REFERENCES

Ammermann, R.T., 1998, 'Methodological issues in child maltreatment research', in Lutzker, J.R., *Handbook of Child Abuse Research and Treatment*, Plenum Press, New York, pp. 9117–31

Andrews, D.A., 2001, 'Effective Practice Future Directions' in Andrews, D., Hollin, C., Raynor, P., Trotter, C., and Armstrong, B., *Sustaining Effectiveness in Working with Offenders*, Cognitive Centre Foundation, Cardiff, UK

Andrews, D.A., Keissling, J.J., Russell, R.J. and Grant, B.A., 1979, *Volunteers and the One to One Supervision of Adult Probationers*, Ontario Ministry of Correctional Services, Toronto, Canada

Andrews, D.A., Zinger, I., Hoge, R., Bouta, J., Gendreau, P. and Cullen, F., 1990, 'Does Correctional Treatment Work? A clinically relevant, psychologically informed meta-analysis', *Criminology* vol. 28, no. 3, pp. 369–401

Baker, M. and Steiner, J., 1995, 'Solution-Focused Social Work: Metamessages to Students in Higher Education Opportunity Programs', *Social Work*, vol. 40, no. 2, pp. 225–32

Burns, P., 1994, *Pro-social Practices in Community Corrections*, honours thesis, Monash University, Department of Social Work, Melbourne, Australia

Carkhuff, R.R., 1969, *Helping and Human Relations*, Holt Rinehart and Winston, New York, USA

Chadwick, D.L., Hensler, D.J. and Sadler, G.L., 1999, 'The National Call to Action: Moving Ahead', *Child Abuse and Neglect*, vol. 23, no. 10, pp. 1011–18

Compton, B. and Galaway, B., 1999, *Social Work Processes*, Sixth Edition, Dorsey, Homewood

DeJong, P. and Miller, S., 1996, 'How to interview for client strengths', *Social Work*, vol. 40, no. 6, pp. 729–36

Department of Health, 1995, *Child Protection: Messages From Research*, Her Majesty's Stationery Office Copyright Unit, London, UK

Department of Human Services, 2000, *Department of Human Services Annual Report*, Melbourne, Australia

DeShazer, S., 1988, *Clues: Investigating Solutions in Brief Therapy*, WW Norton, New York, USA

Donelly, A.C., 1999, 'The practice', *Child Abuse and Neglect*, vol. 23, no. 10, pp. 987–94

Ethier, L.S., et al., 2000, 'Impact of a multi-dimensional intervention program applied to families at risk for child neglect', *Child Abuse Review*, vol. 9, pp. 19–36

Farmer, E., 1999, 'Holes in the Safety Net: the Strengths and Weaknesses of Child Protection Procedures', *Child and Family Social Work*, vol. 4(4), pp. 293–302

Fischer, J., 1973, 'Is Casework Effective?: A Review', *Social Work*, vol. 18, pp. 5–20

——1981, 'The Social Work Revolution', *Social Work*, vol. 26, no. 3, pp. 199–207

Fortune, A., 1992, 'Inadequate Resourses' in Reid, W.J., *Task Strategies: An Empirical Approach to Clinical Social Work*, Columbia University Press, New York, pp. 250–79

Gaudin, J.M., Wodarski, J., Atkinson, M. and Avery, S., 2000, *Outcomes of Social Network Interventions with Neglectful Families*, National clearinghouse on child abuse and neglect information, Washington DC, USA

Gibbons, J., 2001, 'Effective Practice: Social Work's Long History of Concern about Outcomes', *Australian Social Work*, vol. 54, no. 3, pp. 3–15

Gibbs, J., 2001, 'Maintaining Front-Line Workers in Child Protection: A Case for Refocusing Supervision', *Child Abuse Review*, vol. 10, no. 5, pp. 323–35

Gilligan, R., 2001, *Promoting Resilience: A Resource Guide on Working with Children in the Care System*, British Agencies for Adoption and Fostering, London, UK

Gough, D., 1993, *Child Abuse Interventions: A Review of the Research Literature*, Public Health Research Unit, University of Glasgow, London, UK

Gough, D. and Lynch, M., 2002, 'Culture and Child Protection', *Child Abuse Review*, vol. 11, pp. 341–4

——2002b, 'Making Assumptions', *Child Abuse Review*, vol. 11, pp. i–iii

Gray, S., Higgs, M. and Pringle, K., 1997, 'User centred responses to child sexual abuse—the way forward', *Child and Family Social Work*, vol. 2, pp. 49–57

Hallett, C., 1993, 'Working Together in Child Protection', in Waterhouse, L. (Editor), *Child Abuse and Child Abusers: Protection and Prevention*, Kingsley Publishers Ltd, Philadelphia, USA

——1995, *Interagency Co-ordination in Child Protection*, Her Majesty's Stationery Office, London, UK

Harkness, D. and Hensley, H., 1991, 'Changing the focus of social work supervision: effects on client satisfaction and generalised contentment', *Social Work*, vol. 36, no. 6, pp. 506–12

Heatherington, R., Cooper, A., Smith, P. and Wilford, G., 1997, *Protecting Children: Messages from Europe*, Random House Publishing, Lyme Regis, UK

Hepworth, D., Rooney, R. and Larson, J., 2002, *Direct Social Work Practice Theory and Skills*, sixth edition, Brooks Cole, Pacific Grove, Ca., USA

Hetherington, T., 1999, 'Child protection: A new approach in South Australia', *Child Abuse Review*, vol. 8, pp. 120–32

Hohman, M., 1998, 'Motivational Interviewing: An Intervention Tool for Child Welfare Case Workers Working with Substance Abusing Parents', *Child Welfare*, vol. 77, no. 3, pp. 275–89

Holder, R. and Salovitz, B., 2001, *Child Safety and Child Neglect National Resource Centre on Child Maltreatment*, Duluth, GA, USA

Holder, W. and Corey, M., 1986, *Child Protection Services Risk Management: A Decision Making Handbook*, Action for Child Protection, Charlotte, NC, USA

Hood, S., 1997, 'The purchaser/provider separation in child and family social work: Implications for service delivery and for the role of the social worker', *Child and Family Social Work*, vol. 2, pp. 25–35

Howells, J.G., 1974, *Remember Maria*, Butterworth & Co., London, UK

Ife, J., 1997, *Rethinking Social Work*, Longman, Melbourne, Australia

Ivanoff, A., Blythe, B. and Tripodi, T., 1994, *Involuntary Clients in Social Work Practice*, Aldine de Gruyter, New York, USA

Jack, G., 1997, 'Discourses of Child Protection', *British Journal of Social Work*, no. 27, pp. 659–78

Jones, J. and Alcabes, A., 1993, *Client Socialisation: The Achilles Heel of the Helping Professions*, Auburn House, Connecticut, USA

Karamoa, J., Lynch, M. and Kinnair, D., 2002, 'A Continuum of Child Rearing: Responding to Traditional Practices', *Child Abuse Review*, vol. 11, pp. 415–21

Keissling, J., 1982, *The Problem Solving Dimension in Correctional Counselling*, Ontario Ministry of Corrections, Ottawa

Krane, J. and Davies, L., 2000, 'Mothering and Child Protection Practice: Rethinking Risk Assessment', *Child and Family Social Work*, vol. 5(1), pp. 35–45

Laming, Lord, 2003, The Victoria Climbie Inquiry Speech, www.victoria-climbie-inquiry.org.uk

Levey, B., 1999, 'The Call to Action', *Child Abuse and Neglect*, vol. 23, no. 10, pp. 995–1002

Lieberman, M., Yalom, I. and Miles, M., 1973, *Encounter Groups First Facts*, Basic Books, New York, USA

Littlechild, B., 1998, 'Does Family Support Ensure the Protection of Children', *Child Abuse Review*, vol. 7, pp. 116–28

Macdonald, G., 2001, *Effective Interventions in Child Abuse and Neglect*, Wiley, Chichester, UK

McMahon, A., 1998, *Damned if you do, Damned if you don't: Working in Child Welfare*, Ashgate, Aldershot, UK

Maluccio, A., Ainsworth, F. and Thoburn, J., 2000, *Child Welfare Outcome Research in the United Kingdom, United States and Australia*, Child Welfare League of America, Washington DC, USA

Masters, J., Thomas, G., Hollon, S. and Rimm, D., 1987, *Behaviour Therapy*, Harcourt Brace Publishers, Florida, USA

Moyers, T. and Rollnick, S., 2002, 'A Motivational Interviewing Perspective on Resistance to Therapy', *JCLP/In Session: Psychotherapy in Practice*, vol. 58, no. 2, pp. 185–93

Nugent, W.R. and Halvorson, H., 1995, 'Testing the Effects of Active Listening', *Research on Social Work Practice*, vol. 5, no. 2, pp. 152–75

O'Hare, T., 1991, 'Integrating research and practice: A framework for implementation', *Social Work*, vol. 36, no. 3, pp. 220–3

Parton, N. and O'Byrne, P., 2000, *Constructive Social Work: Towards a New Practice*, St Martin's Press, New York, USA

Parton, N., Thorpe, D. and Wattam, C., 1997, *Child Protection Risk and Moral Order*, Basingstoke, Macmillan Press, UK

Pease, R. and Fook, J. (Editors) 1999, 'Transforming Social Work Practice', Allen & Unwin, Sydney, Australia

Pelzer, D., 1997, *The Lost Boy*, pp. 311–12 Orion, London, UK

Perlman, H.H., 1957, *Social Casework: A Problem Solving Process*, University of Chicago Press, Chicago, USA

Pollio, D.E., 1995, 'Use of humour in crisis intervention', *Families in Society*, vol. 76, no. 6, pp. 376–84

Reid, W., 1992, *Task Strategies: An Empirical Approach to Clinical Social Work*, Columbia University Press, USA

——1997, 'Evaluating the dodo's verdict. Do all interventions have equivalent outcomes?', *Social Work Research*, vol. 21, no. 1, pp. 5–16

Reid, W. and Hanrahan, P., 1981, 'Recent Evaluations of Social Work: Grounds for Optimism', *Social Work*, vol. 27, pp. 328–40

Reid, W. and Shyne, A. 1969, *Brief and Extended Casework*, Columbia University Press, New York

Rey, L.D., 1996, 'What social workers need to know about client violence', *Families in Society*, vol. 77, no. 1, pp. 33–9

Rooney, R., 1992, *Strategies for Work with Involuntary Clients*, Columbia University Press, New York, USA

Rothman, J., 1991, 'A model of case management: Towards empirically based practice', *Social Work*, vol. 36, no. 6, pp. 337–43

Rubin, A., 1985, 'Practice effectiveness: More grounds for optimism', *Social Work*, vol. 30 pp. 469–76

Saleebey, D., 2001, 'Practicing the Strengths Perspective: Everyday Tools and Resources', *Families in Society: The Journal of Contemporary Human Services*, vol. 82, no. 3

Schene, P., 1995, *Outcome Measures in Public Child Welfare*, Colorado University, Denver Center for the Study of Social Policy, Denver, USA

Sheldon, B., 1987, 'Implementing findings from social work effectiveness research', *British Journal of Social Work*, vol. 17, pp. 573–86

——2001, 'The Validity of Evidence-Based Practice in Social Work:

A reply to Stephen Webb', *British Journal Of Social Work*, vol. 31, pp. 801–9

Shulman, L., 1991, *Interactional Social Work Practice*, FE Peacock, Illinois, USA

Sinclair, R., 1998, 'Research Review—Involving children in planning their care', *Child and Family Social Work*, vol. 3, pp. 137–42

Siporin, M., 1984, 'Have you heard the one about social work humour', *Social Casework*, vol. 68, no. 8, pp. 459–64

Skehill, C., O'Sullivan, E. and Buckley. H., 1999, 'The nature of child protection: an Irish case study', *Child and Family Social Work*, vol. 4, pp. 145–52

Smokowski, P. and Wodarski, J., 1996, 'Effectiveness of child welfare services', *Research on Social Work Practice*, vol. 6, no. 4, pp. 504–23

Stanley, J. and Goddard, C., 1997, 'Failures in Child Protection: A Case Study', *Child Abuse Review*, vol. 6, pp. 46–54

——2002, *In the Firing Line*, Wiley, Chichester, UK

Swenson, C. and Hanson, R., 1998, 'Sexual Abuse of Children' in Lutzker, J.R., *Handbook of Child Abuse Research and Treatment*, Plenum Press, New York, USA

Thorpe, D., 1994, *Evaluating Child Protection*, Open University Press, Buckingham, UK

Triseliotis, J., Borland, M., Hill, M. and Lambert, L., 1998, 'Social Work Supervision of Young People', *Child and Family Social Work*, vol. 3, pp. 22–35

Trotter, C., 1990, 'Probation Can Work, A Research Study Using Volunteers', *Australian Journal Of Social Work*, vol. 43, no. 2, pp. 13–8

——1993, *The Effective Supervision of Offenders*, unpublished PhD thesis, LaTrobe University, Melbourne, Australia

——1996, 'The Impact of Different Supervision Practices in Community Corrections', *Australian and New Zealand Journal of Criminology*, vol. 29, no. 1, pp. 29–46

——1999, *Working with Involuntary Clients*, Allen & Unwin, Australia

——2002, 'Worker style and client outcome in child protection', *Child Abuse Review*, vol. 11, pp. 38–50

US Department of Health and Human Services, 2001, *Child Maltreatment 2001 Summary of Key Findings*, National Clearinghouse on Child Abuse and Neglect Information, Washington DC, USA

Videka Sherman, L., 1988, 'Meta-analysis of research on social work practice in mental health', *Social Work*, vol. 33, no. 4, pp. 323–38

Webb, S., 2001, 'Some Considerations of the Validity of Evidence-based Practice in Social Work', *British Journal of Social Work*, vol. 31, pp. 57–79

Webster Stratton, C., 1998, 'Parent Training with Low Income Families' in Lutzker, J.R., *Handbook of Child Abuse Research and Treatment*, Plenum Press, New York, USA

White, M. and Epston, D., 1989, *Narrative Means to Therapeutic Ends*, Dulwich Centre Publications, Adelaide, Australia

Wood, M., 1978, 'Casework Effectiveness: A New Look at the Research Evidence', *Social Work*, vol. 23, no. 6, pp. 437–59

INDEX